Praise for Jono Bacon and *People Powered*

If you want to tap into the power that communities can bring to businesses and teams, there is no greater expert than Jono Bacon.

—Nat Friedman, CEO, GitHub

If you want to unlock the power of collaboration in communities, companies, and teams, Jono Bacon should be your tour guide, and *People Powered* should be your map.

—Jamie Smith, Former Deputy Press
Secretary to Barack Obama

Technology tears down the barriers of collaboration and connects our communities—globally and locally. We need to give all organizations and developers the tools to build and foster this effort. Jono Bacon's book provides timely insight into what makes us tick as humans, and how to build richer, stronger technology communities together.

—Kevin Scott, Executive VP and
Chief Technology Officer, Microsoft

Harnessing the collaborative power of communities is critical not just to the success of our businesses but also for our democracy. *People Powered* provides the clear blueprint for producing that success.

—Ali Velshi, Anchor, MSNBC

Communities are a powerful component in digital transformation, and *People Powered* provides the formula.

—Juan Olaizola, COO, Santander España

If you don't like herding cats but need to build a community, you need to read *People Powered*.

—Jamie Hyneman, Cohost and Creator, *Mythbusters*

Jono is an expert at integrating the potential of communities with businesses. *People Powered* provides a clear and thoughtful blueprint for others looking to tap into this potential and unlock benefits for their own organizations.

—Jim Whitehurst, President and CEO, Red Hat;
Author, *The Open Organization*

In my profession, building networks is all about nurturing relationships for the long term. Jono Bacon has authored the recipe on how to do this, and you should follow it.

—Gia Scinto, Head of Talent, Y Combinator Continuity

Communities are the future of business, technology, and collaboration. Jono Bacon's experience, approach, and candor is critical reading for harnessing this future.

—Jim Zemlin, Executive Director,
The Linux Foundation

If you want to harness the power of your customers, *People Powered* should be the first book you open. Highly recommended.

—Whitney Bouck, COO, HelloSign

Jono Bacon has spent years perfecting the craft of building productive communities. *People Powered* is an enormously valuable North Star for doing this work well.

—Villi Iltchev, Partner, August Capital

Community is fundamental to DigitalOcean's success and helped us build a much deeper connection with our audience and customers. *People Powered* presents the simple, pragmatic recipe for doing this well.

—Ben Uretsky, Cofounder, DigitalOcean

When people who are not under your command or payment eagerly work together toward a greater purpose, you can move mountains. Jono Bacon is one of the most accomplished experts on this, and in this book he tells you how it's done.

—Mårten Mickos, CEO, HackerOne

People Powered equips businesses with a powerful community-building formula. It is clear, consistent, and thus a genuinely effective tool for integrating community into the day-to-day operations of a business. Highly recommended.

—Paul Salnikow, CEO,
The Executive Centre

People Powered is a phenomenal guide to creating impact by uniting people around a shared vision, filled with incredibly useful insights and tools for building a powerful community.

—Paul Bunje, Cofounder,
Conservation X Labs

Every business needs to read *People Powered*, not just to build communities but also to build happier, more efficient teams.

—Uttam Tripathi, Head of Global Programs,
DevRel Ecosystem, Google

People Powered is a refreshing and forthright presentation of the state of the art in community building for organizational success.

—Christopher Mondini, VP, Global Stakeholder
Engagement, ICANN

People Powered demystifies the art and science of how to build communities that work. It is essential reading for any organization.

—Dries Buytaert, Founder, Drupal and Acquia

Jono Bacon is the industry leader in community strategy. *People Powered* is the industry-leading approach. Read it.

—Jose Morales, Head of Field Operations, Atlassian

The power of community is proven to us every day in our work with Open Source, Blockchain, and our own Core Community, where Jono has participated. Everywhere he engages and everyone he connects with benefits, which proves why he's recognized as the leader in community development.

—Michael Skok, Founding Partner, Underscore. VC

People Powered sets the record straight about what business or product-related communities are, and the impact you can expect when they are managed well. A must-read for marketers with all levels of experience.

—Billy Cina, Cofounder and CEO, Marketing Envy

Whether you are a start-up or a corporation, if you are not building a community, you are missing an enormous opportunity. *People Powered* needs to be on every executive's bookshelf.

—Maxx Bricklin, Cofounder, BOLD Capital Partners

Communities are powerful, but they need careful management and fostering. Jono Bacon's approach is carefully crafted and thoughtful, yet bold and impactful. Be sure to follow his guidance.

—Dusty Gustafsson, Head of Engagement,
Glorious Games Group

Managing inclusive communities is a key requirement for all future leaders. Jono Bacon provides the leading experience, nuance, and candor for building powerful, engaging, and inclusive communities. Highly recommended reading.

—Nithya Ruff, Senior Director,
Open Source Office, Comcast

I've had the privilege of working with Jono while building community in multiple companies, and his expertise is unrivaled in this space. *People Powered* is a must-read (and reread) for my entire team.

—Joel Carnes, President and CEO,
Alliance for Innovation

At Stack Overflow and Discourse, we didn't just build products for the community; we built products alongside the community. Sharing power with your community and working together toward a common goal is exactly what *People Powered* is about.

—Jeff Atwood, Cofounder,
Stack Overflow and Discourse

Communities require enormous amounts of nuance to get it right, and *People Powered* distills this nuance down logically and clearly. Jono looks at those networks of human brains through many insightful angles, from animal behaviors to the very human need of belonging and connecting to something bigger than yourself.

—Giorgio Regni, Chief Technical Officer, Scality

What makes us unique as a species is that we seem to have an infinite ability to collaborate, from hundreds to millions of people. Collaboration, I believe, is the key to our ability as a species to solve planetary-scale challenges. *People Powered* provides a roadmap for us to further unlock our potential as individuals, to scale collaboration, and to increase our own personal impact.

—Ryan Bethencourt, CEO, Wild Earth;
Partner, Babel Ventures

PEOPLE **POWERED**

PEOPLE
POWERED

HOW COMMUNITIES CAN SUPERCHARGE
YOUR BUSINESS, BRAND, AND TEAMS

JONO **BACON**

HARPERCOLLINS
LEADERSHIP

AN IMPRINT OF HARPERCOLLINS

Published by HarperCollins Leadership, an imprint of HarperCollins Focus LLC.

Any Internet addresses, phone numbers, or company or product information printed in this book are offered as a resource and are not intended in any way to be or to imply an endorsement by HarperCollins Leadership, nor does HarperCollins Leadership vouch for the existence, content, or services of these sites, phone numbers, companies, or products beyond the life of this book.

Book design by Maria Fernandez, Neuwirth & Associates.

ISBN 978-1-4002-1489-1 (eBook)
ISBN 978-1-4002-1488-4 (HC)
ISBN 978-1-4002-1920-9 (ITPE)

Library of Congress Cataloging-in-Publication Data

Names: Bacon, Jono, author. | Bacon, Jono.
Title: People powered : how communities can supercharge your business, brand, and teams / Jono Bacon.
Description: Nashville : HarperCollins Leadership, 2019.
Identifiers: LCCN 2019007469 (print) | LCCN 2019020210 (ebook) | ISBN 9781400214891 (e-book) | ISBN 9781400214884 (hardback)
Subjects: LCSH: Customer loyalty. | Customer services. | Branding (Marketing) | Electronic villages (Computer networks)
Classification: LCC HF5415.525 (ebook) | LCC HF5415.525 .B33 2019 (print) | DDC 658.8/343--dc23
LC record available at https://lccn.loc.gov/2019007469

Printed in the United States of America
19 20 21 22 23 LSC 5 4 3 2 1

For Erica and Jack.

You have taught me more about humanity than you will ever know.

Contents

Acknowledgments

This book wouldn't have been possible without a number of people.

First, thanks to the crack team of literary blackbelts at HarperCollins Leadership for taking this project on. This includes my fantastic editor, Sara Kendrick, as well as Tim Burgard, Jeff James, Hiram Centeno, Sicily Axton, Natalie Nyquist, and Amanda Bauch. I am also enormously grateful to my agent, Margot Hutchinson at Waterside Productions, Inc., for her belief in the potential for this book and my PR team at Smith PR.

Like anything in life, it takes a village. A number of people took time from their work, families, and interests to help me hammer my raw material into the product you are holding in your hands. This includes Stuart Langridge, Kerri Pike Knapp, Stephen Walli, Ilan Rabinovich, Jeremy Garcia, Mårten Mickos, Neil Levine, and my dad, John Bacon.

Many thanks to Peter Diamandis, Joseph Gordon-Levitt, Jim Whitehurst, Ali Velshi, Mike Shinoda, Noah Everett, Jim Zemlin, Alexander van Engelen, and others who also generously shared their insight. Your wisdom helped strengthen the core message of this book.

I am eternally thankful to my family and friends for all the love and support you provide. Thanks to Erica and Jack Bacon, John, Polly, Simon, and Martin Bacon, Joe, Adam, and Danielle Brescia, Sue and Vance Smith, Dalene and Mark Ruhe, Mindy Faieta, Adam Hoffert, Lee Reilly, Federico Lucifredi, Jorge Castro, Tom Draper, Guy Martin, Todd Lewis, and the many more I am leaving out like the inconsiderate clod that I am.

Finally, thanks to my fantastic jonobacon.com members.[1] Thanks to the thousands of you who I have met over the years on the road and at home: you helped shape my ideas, improve my work and approach, and inspired me to keep learning. There are far too many of you to name, but you all played a critical role in my world. Thanks!

Foreword

I t always amazes me what we can achieve when we try to make the impossible possible.

Shortly after finishing medical school at Harvard, I read about the twenty-five-thousand-dollar Orteig Prize in Charles Lindbergh's autobiography, *Spirit of St. Louis*.[1] The competition launched in 1919 and challenged intrepid aviators to fly an airplane nonstop between New York and Paris, a feat that at the time seemed nearly impossible.

As history has continually taught us though, the human spirit has the courage to look adversity squarely in the eye. The prize was won in 1927 by Charles Lindbergh following his heroic 33.5-hour flight, and it significantly advanced aviation technology.

I was enormously inspired by this story and the power of incentive prizes—so much so that I launched the first XPRIZE in 1996. This brought the spirit of the Orteig Prize into the modern era, offering a $10 million purse to the first team able to build and fly a reusable spacecraft capable of carrying three adults to one hundred kilometers above the earth twice in two weeks.

Just like the Orteig prize, when the XPRIZE was announced, the idea of a private team building and flying human-carrying spaceships looked like an impossible feat. Eight years later, on October 4, 2004, the $10 million Ansari XPRIZE for spaceflight was won by Scaled Composites and their winning vehicle, Space-ShipOne, an event that would fuel a new age of commercial space travel.

While these were two different incentive prizes in two different eras, there was one clear pattern running through both: the right mixture of opportunity, potential, and a grit to succeed created a combination able to produce exponential innovation and results.

This mixture is formed of fundamentally human ingredients, which manifest in the incredible work I have seen across the many other XPRIZEs that followed: global literacy, medicine, artificial intelligence, ocean health and mapping, transportation, oil-spill cleanup, and beyond.

I believe communities are increasingly critical in scaling up this potential and fostering a new era of how we innovate. Our world is becoming more connected every day. In 2017 3.8 billion people were online, and by 2024—via ground-based 5G, atmospheric satellites, and thousands of orbiting satellites—we will connect all eight billion humans on Earth.[2] The impact of a globally connected species is far more exciting because each of us now has a computer in our pockets that is millions of times cheaper, millions of times more powerful, and thousands of times smaller than the computers that got humanity to the Moon in 1969.[3]

This reality is producing conditions like never before for people across the globe to collaborate, share information, and build new things. Innovation is no longer just happening in labs. It is getting created on the Internet, at meetups, in STEM classes, and in communities around the world.

This combination of connectivity and technology is going to be the catalyst for our next generation of innovators to rise, bolstered by a global community that understands them and supports their growth, experimentation, and success. To harness this potential we need to understand communities: how they work and how to produce thriving environments that are productive and inclusive. This is complicated and has historically been something of a "black art" to master the right balance of people, process, and technology that constitutes a successful community.

Jono has been a global leader in community strategy for years. He has spent his entire career focused on understanding the countless nuances of how to build communities and integrate them into businesses. The book you are holding provides his blueprint and approach, one formed from his work across many businesses and sectors.

I hope you harness our inbuilt human potential to produce communities that can further innovate, inspire, and deliver your own exponential results. We don't make a brighter future alone; we make it together.

Here's to making the impossible possible.

Peter H. Diamandis, MD
Founder & Executive Chairman, XPRIZE Foundation
Executive Founder, Singularity University
December 2018

CHAPTER 1

What Is a Community and Why Do You Need to Build One?

If you want to go quickly, go alone. If you want to go far, go together.

—African proverb

In 2006, at the tender age of twenty-six, I started a new job at a British company called Canonical. Founded by newly minted South African millionaire Mark Shuttleworth, the company was focused on building a competitor to Microsoft's Windows operating system monopoly. The twist was that this new operating system, Ubuntu, was created by a globally connected network of volunteers who freely shared the open-source code. My role was to turn a small set of contributors into an international movement.

Less than a year into my new gig I got an enthusiastic email from a kid called Abayomi. Little did I realize this message would have a transformative impact not just on my career but on the rest of my life.

Abayomi lived in a rural village in Africa. Like many young people, his email was disjointed, yet sweet. He talked about how he discovered Ubuntu, how he tried to explain it to his parents, and how he struggled to participate in the community due to not having a computer at home. His family lived a frugal life, but his interest in technology was something his parents wanted to support, despite their limited means.

He told me how he would perform chores around his village all week to earn as much money as he could. He would then walk two hours to his local town and use the money he earned to buy time at an Internet cafe to participate in the Ubuntu community.

This Internet time was usually short, often less than an hour. He would answer questions from users, write documentation and help guides, translate Ubuntu into his local language, and more. Then he would walk the two hours back home. He didn't complain; he didn't whine. Quite the opposite—he gushed with enthusiasm about how he felt energized that he, a kid in rural Africa, could play a role in a global project making a real difference. I was stunned at not just his commitment but his humility.

Back then, in 2007 in England, Abayomi's email was yet another example of a rebellion against what I was seeing where I lived. People often complained about their communities withering and dying. It was the same scripture churned out each time: "People don't know their neighbors anymore," and "People spend all their time buried in movies, video games, and the Internet." Lather, rinse, and repeat.

Yet here I saw people such as Abayomi joining and thriving in communities that had an impact. These were communities that were both global and local at the same time. *They delivered swathes of meaning, not just to the participants, but also to the organizations that facilitated them.* Our friend in Africa was just one cog in a machine that was growing around the world.

His email made two things clear to me. First, *human beings are naturally social animals.* We have been for hundreds of thousands of years. Yet something magical was happening. This delicious cocktail of technology, connectivity, and people was creating the ability for thousands around the world to come together as a well-oiled (and often rather caffeinated) machine to generate incredible value, far beyond the capabilities of any individual. Abayomi's passion for the Ubuntu community wasn't just that he could make an impact; *his impact was amplified when combined with other people in the community.*

I knew then and there that my life's work would be to understand every damn nuance of how this cocktail works. I wanted to understand not only the tech but also the people, the psychology, the emotional driving forces . . . anything that could help me to understand how these pieces worked together and what makes the people involved tick. I wasn't interested in shortcuts. I was interested in understanding how all the pieces click together.

Second, I knew that my responsibility as a community leader was to make sure that Abayomi got the *maximum value* out of his hour at that Internet cafe. If he went above and beyond to get there, I needed to go above and beyond to make it as rewarding as possible. He, and thousands of others, deserved it.

A QUIET REVOLUTION

The scripture about communities dying was not entirely generational grumblings about the young guns.

Historically, communities used to be distinctly local in nature: they existed in your region, in your town, and potentially even on your street. They manifested in local book clubs, knitting circles, political meetings, gaming clubs, and more. They took place in church halls, schools, and coffee shops. They were often attended by enthusiasts and sometimes by nosy busybodies. New members were typically recruited by bringing friends, word of mouth, posters displayed in businesses, and free ads in the local paper.

These communities were engaging, high-touch, and meaningful, but they had their limitations. There was a limited audience available to attract, and even if you did get people through the door, there were only so many that you could fit into the physical venue.

Not only this, but *joining these groups required quite a leap for newcomers.* You were asking people to take time away from their families, friends, and colleagues to show up and talk to a bunch of people they didn't know. This was a tough pill to swallow for many, particularly those who were anxious meeting new people or those in underrepresented groups.

Even if you did pluck up the courage to go to one of these community meetings, there was no guarantee it would be fun or interesting. While some were a fun, dynamic meeting of minds (such as sports fans getting together), some were dry, awkward discussions. These groups often reflected the personality of their founders. The fun ones were generally founded by fun people.

If you made it to the end, after the meeting there would often be no continuation until the next time everyone was back together in person. People would go home and there would be little-to-no communication until they reconvened in the same building the next week or month. It didn't feel like a community as much as a series of events that tended to attract the same crowd over and over again.

This blend of limitations often nixed the potential of many of these local communities. They were often local curiosities that served a niche audience. Unsurprisingly, some of these communities started to die out, likely contributing to the grumbling from the elder generations about how community wasn't a thing anymore. Oh, and to get those damn kids off their carefully manicured lawns.

THE MICROCHIP AND THE MODEM: THEY FIGHT CRIME

Aside from the '90s bringing us hammer pants, bleached spiky haircuts, and awful skateboard movies, we also started seeing the world become more connected.

While the Internet was forged in universities and research campuses in the '80s and '90s, it was far too expensive and technical for the general public to use. As the tech became simpler, it became more pervasive.

People want to engage and connect with each other. We want to build relationships. We want to share ideas, information, and creativity. Unsurprisingly, early communities started forming like clustered amoebas in this rudimentary online pond.

In the '80s, early message boards formed on bulletin board systems such as CompuServe and distributed discussion systems such as Usenet, covering a raft of primarily academic and rather nerdy pursuits.[1] People produced and shared text files containing anything from scientific research, to technology guides, to various acts of anarchy (such as making backyard explosives and pranking your local burger joint).[2]

This fascinated the early digital explorers. For those technically inclined enough to get connected (often at universities), this global network provided a way to communicate with people on the other side of the country or world. You could discover information that would never be in your local library. *It made information and those who produced it powerful.*

Given that the early Internet pipes were thin enough to only exchange small chunks of text, these early communities optimized for the best kind of text. One kind was source code, the building blocks and recipe of software.

Back in those early days, software was a closed-off world. Large companies such as IBM, Apple, and Microsoft produced software and kept their code such a carefully guarded secret that the fried-chicken Colonel would be jealous. While this was the norm, one person—Richard Stallman, furious that he couldn't fix his printer software (because the code wasn't available)—believed that *all* software code should be free for people to share and improve.

Stallman kicked off the GNU community, who started making free software and sharing the code on the Internet.[3] It was a magical combination: most of the people online back then were techies and programmers. People started to download this code, which was simply digital text, improve it, and share their results with others of a nerdy persuasion. A small library of free tools started to build. This jump-started other communities such as Linux, Apache, Debian, and more.

The Internet became a place where people didn't just consume knowledge and have discussions; it was also a place where people could build things together. This set off a chain reaction. People built software, shared knowledge, produced educational materials, started websites, and more. Just like Abayomi would experience years later, *for every person who contributed, it made the global community even more powerful.* The power of the group was getting stronger and stronger.

While the tech was interesting, it was the people and communities that powered this creation that fascinated me. We were getting a taste of what was possible when people connected together digitally, accessed the same tools, and participated in a central community that generated meaningful value for everyone involved.

FIVE FOUNDATIONAL COMMUNITY TRENDS

If we were to slide any of those early communities under a microscope, we would see five important trends. These underscore everything you are going to read throughout this book, and they are the foundation for the incredible value that can be driven by businesses, organizations, and individuals who want to harness them.

1. Access to a Growing, Globally Connected Audience

Unlike the local church group, today we have the opportunity to access a truly global audience. If there are people out there who share your interest, you can build a community. Cheap marketers simply spam this audience, but we are smarter than that. We are going to engage with them, build relationships, and generate and share value together.

2. Cheap Commodity Tools for Providing Access

You can access and harness this global audience with readily available, affordable tools. Heck, you could start a community with free web hosting, a free forum, and free social media networks. The tools are not the most interesting part of the community equation; it is how we weave them into the ways people share and collaborate.

3. Immediate Delivery of Broad Information and Expertise

Unlike the old weekly meeting at the local community center, this global audience is immediately addressable. We can share news, information, education, and more. We can get the word out more quickly and easily than ever before, stay in touch, and build relationships electronically and in person.

4. Diversified Methods of Online Collaboration

As technology (and our broader understanding of it) evolves, we are figuring out new and interesting ways to work together. In days of old we simply shared content. Today we can work together and collaborate around content and education, be it coding software, building hardware, writing books, making music, creating art, and more.

5. Most Important: A Growing Desire for Meaningful, Connected Work

This is the core of why communities tick. Spin all the way back to the very first page of this, the very first chapter of this book. Do you know why Abayomi walked for hours to his local Internet café? It was because the work was *meaningful* for him. He could have an *impact*. While physically he was a kid in the middle of Africa, digitally he was a global player in a movement for a greater good. Abayomi is not alone. This desire is intrinsic to the human condition, and we can harness it in our communities.

A LOUDER REVOLUTION

These five trends have been the foundation behind some impressive communities in recent years, many of which are from recognized brands such as Salesforce, Lego, Procter & Gamble, and Nintendo.

These communities include users coming together to share information and guidance for others using a product, champions who actively create and consume content that promotes the success of the product or organization, and even groups of producers and creators who collaborate independently (often in conjunction with an organization's employees) to build real, measurable value via derivative products and services.

In all of these cases, these communities are comprised of bright-eyed, enthusiastic volunteers who really care about those brands and products. No one is on the payroll, yet they do amazing work, consistently building broader brand awareness, creating content, and providing a home for likeminded users and customers. This includes:

- Random House, who built the 300,000-member-strong Figment community, which shares, creates, moderates, and recommends content related to Random House products.[4]
- Lego Ideas, an official community from the Lego Group, in which nearly 1 million members have submitted ideas for new Lego sets (many of which get produced and sold), provided support, and participated in contests.[5]
- XBOX Live, in which its 59 million active members play, chat, and collaborate together around their favorite video games.[6]
- The *SAP Community Network*, in which their 2.5 million membership advocate, support, and integrate SAP products.[7]
- Procter & Gamble, who launched a community for teenage girls to get answers to their (at times awkward to ask) questions, which has expanded across twenty-four countries.[8]
- Wikipedia, entirely built by a community of writers, which has created more than 22 million articles across 285 languages (and is valued at $6.6 billion by the Smithsonian).[9]
- The broader Open Source community, which has built technology that powers the majority of consumer devices, data centers, the cloud, and the Internet itself.[10]

While Emmy Award–winner Joseph Gordon-Levitt is known to many as an actor in movies and shows such as *Looper, Snowden,*

Lincoln, Inception, (500) Days of Summer, 50/50, and *3rd Rock from the Sun,* he is also the founder of HITRECORD—an online creative platform he started with his brother, Dan, in 2005.

HITRECORD provides a place where artists of all kinds can create art together, emphasizing collaboration over self-promotion. Projects are started by members of HITRECORD's worldwide community of seven hundred thousand artists creating pieces such as short films, songs, and books together.[11] Anyone can participate by remixing and building upon each other's contributions bit-by-bit. HITRECORD's unique collaborative process has yielded a wide range of partnerships with top-tier brands, multiple publishing deals, screenings at international film festivals, and an Emmy-winning television series.[12]

Joseph shared with me how the community has evolved:[13]

Back in 2005, HITRECORD was never contemplated as a collaborative platform. It started out as a simple message board, but as people used it, we realized people didn't only want to watch my stuff, they wanted to make stuff together. When we saw that happening, my brother and I thought that was so cool. He was the coder, and started building more features on top of this message board to encourage the collaborative process. Then, slowly, the community grew, and after a few years I started working with a couple friends of mine to turn this community into a production company.

Joe and his brother tapped into two key drivers of artists: the desire to collaborate and to have their art recognized.

HITRECORD doesn't just provide a rewarding way to make art with others, but everyone whose contribution is included in a final funded HITRECORD production is compensated (to date, nearly $3 million has been paid to the community).[14] The value was clear.

New businesses often see particularly interesting value in community. As an example, Star Citizen, a popular multiplayer space combat game used Kickstarter to raise $500,000 to build their game and have subsequently raised $150,000,000 in crowd-funded donations and have built a community of 1.8 million players.[15]

Other companies have used community growth as an opportunity to build market relevance, such as the cloud infrastructure company, Docker, who started out life relatively unknown, but built a passionate community around its technology that helped them to subsequently become a staple in the technology infrastructure industry. They are now valued at $1 billion.[16]

This is an enormous opportunity, particularly for new businesses. A well-designed and run community can generate an army of ground troops that will help you pierce through the noise into relevance.

The inverse of these community opportunities are of course, community threats, and many companies who have not taken a strategic approach to community have struggled with ecosystem growth and engagement. This has included the troubled relationship Uber has faced with their driver community, challenges that United has faced with customer satisfaction and engagement, and the exodus of community members from MySpace and Digg, partially due to changing fashions, but also due to a lack of incentivization and engagement.[17] Sadly, it also includes difficulties faced by popular video games with abusive behavior from participants in online games.[18]

Effective community strategy is not merely an antidote to these difficulties, it is preventative medicine. It provides a structured way in which to define your audience, understand how to serve them efficiently and effectively, deliver the right tools to help them succeed, better support them, channel their feedback to improve your product, and thus reduce the risk of frustration and people leaving.

Now, the psychological and behavioral drivers that generate this value are not unique to public communities. More and more companies, particularly large-scale businesses, have been building internal communities within the walls of their organization to drive efficiencies in product development, reduce team silos, improve communication, provide collaboration and career opportunities, expand recruiting, and to support happier, more fulfilled employees. This has included PayPal, Facebook, Bosch, Microsoft, Capital One, and Google. Similarly, everything you read in this book can be applied to both public and private communities.

Let's start at the beginning and look at what communities are and why they are interesting.

WHAT ARE COMMUNITIES?

OK, let's hit reverse a little. There is clearly a bunch of opportunity buried in your common or garden-variety community, but . . . well . . . what exactly is a community?

Fundamentally, they are *groups of people united by a common interest.* They can be as small as a local book club that meets in a coffee shop on Tuesday evenings, or as big as a global community comprised of millions of users spread all over the world. They can be online, in-person, or a mixture of both. They can be formal and focused or loose and ad hoc.

Unlike other groups of people who gather together, such as audiences watching a rock concert, employees commuting to a large organization's campus, or customers standing in line for the latest gizmo on launch day, *communities have a greater degree of permanence between participants and activities they engage in.*

When the rock concert ends, the show is over. Communities are different. They provide a place where people can get together to repeatedly engage and possibly collaborate with each other. This forms a connective tissue between those people and the broader community. In much the same way muscle is formed when you repeat the same motions, community is formed when people engage together more and more.

Fractal Audio Systems, based in New Hampshire, builds a range of equipment designed for guitarists. They are known for their high-quality emulation of analog tube amplifiers, and they have developed a considerable community around their products.[19]

Arguably, a typical Fractal Audio Systems customer could buy their products, download a few sound patches and updates, and be on their way. Instead, their forty-thousand-strong community discusses and supports each other extensively on their forum, produces sounds that others can download (via their Axe Change service), and has produced a raft of documentation, videos, tutorials, and more for how to use the products as effectively as possible.[20]

Fractal Audio Systems doesn't just have a customer-base; they have a rapidly evolving and growing community whose members keep coming back to the well. This is not just because they get more out of the products, but because they love the sense of *belonging* the community provides. I am one of those members.

The Fundamentals

Now, as we are starting to get to know each other, I need to make two things clear to you.

First, I am going to be bluntly honest with you all. *There is no silver bullet or guarantee that your community is going to succeed.* Building communities is *hard*. A major risk of failure exists if you are not integrating community development skills into your teams and thus getting inconsistent, lumpy execution. This book presents my approach and method, which is a pragmatic, practical approach. While it is designed to help mitigate these risks, it is critical that you focus heavily in baking these skills into your organization to help you and your teams succeed.

Second, this is complex work. *There is a lot of detail and as such a high risk of distraction and chasing after shiny things.* We need to stay focused on the right things but always ensure they are connected to our broader objectives.

When I learn any discipline, I zoom all the way out first to see the broader picture we want to paint and then gradually zoom in and fill in the details. This is going to be the approach I take throughout this book. So, let's zoom out and first take a look at the *social* dynamics of how communities work.

If you want to build a great piece of software, you need to understand the hardware it is running on. If you want to be a professional athlete, you need to understand the rules of your game. If you want to be a world-class BBQ cook, you need to understand how your grill works. Similarly, *if you want to build a community, you need to understand the psychology of people and how they engage with each other.*

The Heart of the Human Condition

When you take away the computers, screens, cell phones, and cars, it is easy to forget that we are actually animals.

Just like animals in natural habitats, there are drivers that influence our behavior and how we think and approach the world. These drivers happen deep in our subconscious, but understanding them can provide a psychological blueprint for how we approach building communities that map effectively to the natural human condition.

This is reflected in my Community Belonging Path (Fig. 1.1):

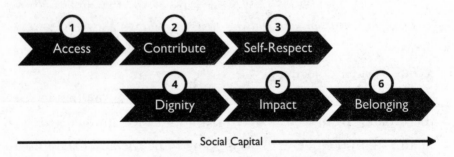

Fig. 1.1: Community Belonging Path

All community success stories start with someone having *access* to the information, tools, permission, and guidance needed to help them *contribute* something as a newcomer to the community. This contribution can come in the form of answering a question, producing content, sharing insight, producing software, or myriad other things. *Simple, available, and intuitive access is essential for a community to succeed.* It is the gateway for everything that follows.

When new contributions offer value to the community (and are generally appreciated), it typically builds a sense of *self-respect* in the individual. They feel they are doing good work that is validated by others, and confidence starts to form. This confidence helps them to more proactively and logically solve problems and foster better social cohesion in the group.

As self-respect grows and they continue to contribute, a sense of *dignity* forms. Dignity is an important psychological sensation. It gives us pride, peace, social acceptance, and an intrinsic sense of value. It continues to build confidence in ourselves and our capabilities. It feels bloody good, and for good reason.

A key input in building a sense of dignity is that the work we do has *meaning.* As a professor of psychology and economics at Duke University, Dan Ariely has studied how meaning plays an essential role in our lives.[21] He uses an example of a banker who produced an extensive PowerPoint presentation that was central to a merger in his bank. While the banker worked on the presentation, he enjoyed his work and was quite happy to work late into the night to perfect it. When the merger was canceled, he felt deflated. He had still done good work that his manager appreciated, but because no one would see it and it wouldn't play a role in the desired merger, it was enormously depressing to him. He felt his work didn't have meaning.

We *need* our work to have meaning, and the communities that succeed the most are clearly able to draw a connection between the work of their members and the broader mission of the overall community. This is why activist groups such as Amnesty International, the Sierra Club, and Black Lives Matter generate so much devotion: their members feel their work has much broader meaning.

Somewhat magically, when we *do* feel our work has meaning, it gives us a turbo boost of confidence to step up and have *impact*. This is where the big, brave ideas come from, emboldened by the respect we now have in the community. This is often where we challenge our assumptions and norms and sail into new territory. Truly world-changing communities are powered by people who feel they have the ability and respect to go out and do something bold because they have both their personal confidence and the shared confidence of the group.

When this pathway is followed successfully, it generates the ultimate psychological treasure in communities: *belonging.* A sense of belonging makes us feel part of something. We feel validated by our social group (the community) that we are needed, respected, and part of the familial unit. We feel we would be missed if we left or even went on vacation. Dignity provides personal satisfaction and peace in the individual. Belonging provides satisfaction and peace within that individual's social circle.

As your members flow through the Community Belonging Path and repeatedly contribute *value* into the shared community, *social capital* is generated. This is an unspoken, unseen value that is attached to each contribution a community member makes. There is no formal number for social capital and there is no platform that counts it. Social capital manifests as the respect the group has for the individual based on their aggregate contributions *and* the tenor in which they engage.

Just like in an economy where money can buy goods and services, *social capital is a key currency in communities.* It is forged from respect, which in turn generates influence. This is how people become leaders in communities: they repeatedly do great work, develop enormous amounts of respect, and as such are trusted by the community to make decisions.

Importantly, social capital isn't just generated by contributing something worthwhile to the community, but in *how* you produce it. If you are kind, respectful, collaborative, and produce great work, you will ooze social capital. If you are an asshole and produce great work, your social capital will be far more limited. The *social* in *social capital* is the magic word.

This Community Belonging Path is what powered Abayomi to walk so far every week and demonstrate such devotion to the Ubuntu community. *Wiring up your community to provide clear, simple access, the ability to contribute effectively, and a sense of dignity and belonging builds success.* It won't just build retention; it will create an infectious level of enthusiasm and commitment that will shape a mature, valuable community.

As you read this book and as we explore the different elements of making communities that tick, always focus on these three key ingredients:

1. How can you make it easy for people to contribute and produce value?
2. How can you help them contribute over and over again and build up their social capital?

3. How can you make them feel welcome and intrinsic to the community while building a sense of belonging?

If you get the *human ingredients* right, the rest is gravy.

VALUE AND OPPORTUNITY

One of the aspects that fascinates me about community strategy is that everything is different and everything is the same. While many of these deep-rooted psychological and social ingredients are floating around in our brains, communities can manifest and deliver vastly different types of value.

If you are like anyone else with a pulse and an idea, you are reading all of this through your own lens. What kind of value can communities offer to you? How can you harness all of this to further your goals?

Let's start with value. There are five major categories of value that most communities tend to generate.

1. Customer and User Engagement

You would have to have a screw loose to not want a close, trusting relationship with your customers and users. These customers and users are the lifeblood that not only put food on the table but bring meaning to your work.

Customer success and delight builds retention and brand loyalty, and it is a critical way to separate yourself from those wannabes who call themselves your competitors. Sadly, this is an area where many businesses struggle, but we can turn this into our own opportunity.

Communities have proven to be a fantastic vessel for building a closer relationship between businesses and customers. A community provides a shared environment where members can build relationships with the company, consume and contribute additional value, and see this value being consumed by other members. This builds goodwill. It creates trust. It builds brand loyalty.

One example is Salesforce. Their Customer Relationship Management (CRM) system is big business, providing a central database platform where businesses track customers, clients, partners, and more. As I scribble these words down, Salesforce is arguably the most popular CRM system in the world. Boasting 150,000 customers and an estimated 3.75 million subscribers, Salesforce has an enormous customer base across a broad range of industries.[22]

The product itself is very comprehensive (some may argue a little *too* comprehensive), with a number of integrated services bolted in. As such, understanding these different services, using the right features, and making it work for the customer can be a steep hill to climb.

To address this, in 2005 the Salesforce Success Community was formed (which was later renamed the Salesforce Trailblazer Community). Initially it provided access to documentation and guidance, but it started steadily mixing a broader range of features into the community mixing bowl to connect with members.[23]

The community featured online help and documentation and showcased new functionality and features in each new release. It provided the go-to resource for customers to stay up to date on the products and how to harness those features. It provided a warm blanket wrapped around the product, which helped customers succeed in using it.

As the community continued to grow, in 2007 they integrated discussion forums and the ability to propose new ideas for features. Power users emerged in the forum and started to break out and form user groups. This success continued into 2008, when community content and features were integrated into their flagship Dreamforce conference (an event that almost brings San Francisco to a standstill due to its size). The community hit its one-million-members mark in 2014.

Since then the Salesforce Trailblazer Community, as it is now known, has provided additional structured methods of tapping into existing expertise as well as engaging with the community around new topics. There is little doubt that the community has played a significant role in the success of Salesforce.

2. Awareness, Marketing, and Customer/User Success

"Eyeballs." That was the answer a friend of mine gave when I asked about her number one goal for the year. Every business needs to grow, and this doesn't just drive the marketing department but also sales, product, partnerships, and more. Communities can provide a powerful vehicle for building buzz and awareness about your product, service, and brand.

The idea is simple: if you don't have a community, you are fully dependent on your marketing and PR teams, which might be just a handful of people. They may be great, but there are only so many hours in the day. If you build an energetic army of fans, when they are harnessed well, they can be dependable ground troops in getting the message out.

These members won't just support and promote your brand, they can generate content that will increase your search engine performance, increase your social media presence, promote the community at local events and global conferences, and open up opportunities with future potential customers, partners, and other engagements. Yep, this all results in the eyeballs my ex-colleague wanted to see.

As an example, back in the early 2000s and early days of the web, a war was brewing. Microsoft had produced the ubiquitous Internet Explorer web browser, but there were concerns that Microsoft would try to lock down the open standards of the web so many sites would not work in other browsers.

The new Mozilla community, forged from the ashes of Netscape, kicked off the GetFirefox community. They advocated for an open web and open standards. They fervently advocated Firefox as a solution for this freer and more-open Internet. As the global community grew, they promoted this message online and in local communities. They were incredibly creative in how they attracted eyeballs. They produced swag, did online promotion, and even produced crop circles and generated enough money to put a full-page ad in the *New York Times*.[24] There is little doubt that this community had a profound impact in the growth of Firefox and, subsequently, an open web.

With the birth of crowdfunding on platforms such as Kickstarter and Indiegogo, community advocacy and promotion has similarly played a pivotal role. Some of the most funded campaigns, such as the Pebble Smartwatch (raising $20 million for their $500k goal) and Exploding Kittens game (raising nearly $9 million for their $10k goal), used community advocacy as a means to reach these goals.[25]

This all results in not just awareness of your product but also of your brand. *Your community can be an amplifier that transmits your brand to a broader set of people.* This has happened with brands such as GitHub, Reddit, Battlefield, Facebook, and more.

3. Education and Support

Products are tricky beasts. You can have the glitziest of glitzy marketing and sales materials in the world, but if your customers and users can't figure out how to use your product, you will lose them. The time between product discovery and clear experienced value has to be short, and the experience has to be simple and pragmatic.

Anyone who has built a product has to deal with how to effectively deliver education and support. The more complex your product gets, the more complex it is to ensure your customers and users are able to understand it and get a good solid chunk of value out of it.

Delivering this education and support can be expensive and time consuming, with most companies producing a library of documentation and videos and providing a support email address. This immediately becomes a cost center, and companies tend to reluctantly invest in it, despite the importance in security for customers.

Communities can be a godsend here. Enthusiastic users of your product or service will often produce guides, documentation, videos, how-tos, and more, all which help to seal this education gap. Not only this, community members will often provide on-tap help and support where prospective and existing customers can ask questions and get help. For example, the game Minecraft has 90 million active monthly users.[26] Many of these players learn the game and how to master it from the Minecraft Forum and Minecraft Wiki, the latter of which has more than forty-five-hundred articles, entirely produced by the community.[27]

If people love your product or service, and it is something that they want to master, it is ripe for this kind of content. All of this taps into a person's natural urge to teach and experience satisfaction when that teaching helps someone to accomplish great results. If we can incentivize and harness this education and support, you will have an incredibly powerful resource on tap for your customers and users.

4. Product and Technology Development

Red Hat is one of the most successful open-source organizations in the world. They were acquired in 2018 by IBM for $34 billion.[28] Since 1993 Red Hat has been actively launching and participating in hundreds of open-source software communities across the cloud, infrastructure, devices, and beyond.

Their CEO, Jim Whitehurst, who is one of the most talented execs I know, firmly sees the importance of community as a catalyst for their innovation. "Our method of working across multiple open-source communities hasn't just allowed us to survive; it's enabled us to actually thrive as new technological shifts have occurred. Our innovative technologies are an output of our organizational culture—our people—who give us the ability to adapt and rebound in the wake of disruptive change."[29]

Red Hat doesn't operate alone. The global open-source community has produced tools such as Linux, Kubernetes, OpenStack, Apache, Debian, Jenkins, GNOME, and others that have had a profound impact on various industries, powering clouds, devices, vehicles, space shuttles, and more.

Why do these companies invest in creating code that is shared freely? There are many reasons. Open code means you can attract new contributors who produce features, fix bugs, and improve the overall security of a product. Freely available access makes it easier for people to try technologies, and many companies run a successful open-core model where they have the free open-source version (the gateway drug) and an enterprise version with additional paid features. Throughout all of this, your brand, technology, and team has a much broader potential audience due to the lower barrier to entry.

All of this can generate significant financial value. As one example, the Linux Foundation, a trade organization focused on open source, determined that to rebuild an open-source operating system using proprietary methodologies would cost $10.8 billion.[30]

Other communities have also formed to create additions that sit on top of existing platforms. The Wordpress content management platform, which is available freely, has developed a passionate community that has built more than thirty-nine thousand plugins and extensions that extend what Wordpress can do. This has resulted in just under a billion downloads and Wordpress running 30 percent of the web.[31]

There are also other types of product development that communities can help with beyond code. Massive online games and environments such as SecondLife and Star Citizen (the latter of which reached $200 million in their crowdfunding campaign) have made content development a central theme.[32] Players can create items, buildings, storylines, and more, many which are intricate and take months of development.

In some of these environments, entire economies are formed from producing and selling this content. In fact, back in 2008 I met a guy in Amsterdam who quit his day job because he ran a number of virtual businesses inside the SecondLife online world. People like him fueled much of the innovation in that community via this economic driver.

If you can think of opportunity, you can probably harness it. In 2007 I wrote an application to help people consume online learning across a range of technology projects. I wrote and released the application, but one limitation was that it was only available in English. I shared it with our community and asked for help to translate it, and within twenty-four hours it was fully translated into eleven languages. Before long, it would be available in forty languages.

Other communities have contributed product feedback and testing, usability, visual design, and more. *If you provide a clear way to map a community member's skills to delivering meaningful work, it is incredible what results you can generate.*

5. Business Capabilities

"I just don't understand why anyone would want to sit in a cube all day and work through a task list," said a young woman whom I spoke to at a university a few years back. I have to say, I agree with her.

She is growing up in an age where collaboration online is the norm. She has enormous control over her own destiny in her chosen career path, and she understands that she can build her experience and résumé on the Internet and via community groups and meetups.

This poses a threat, or at least an awkward reality, to larger businesses. If you don't have an environment that shares similar principles to a collaborative community (cross-team collaboration, career development, social engagement, etc.), you are going to struggle to hire. While the free soda and trail mix may woo employees to work with you, a healthy working environment will keep them.

Building and engaging with a community doesn't just integrate these skills into your organization, it also provides *a funnel of potential candidates*. Many of my clients hire a significant number of people from their communities. This doesn't just make recruitment easier, but the employees also come prebaked with relevant experience and context. For many of these members, their dream job is working for the company. It is a win-win situation.

Communities also provide *a wealth of user experience and insight*. As your community grows and as you build retention in members, they will develop a fantastic corpus of experience and expertise that you should tap into. This expertise and insight can help you with product design, development, and delivery. They can provide insight into how you could continue to grow and optimize the community as well as much-needed honesty (sometimes of the brutal kind). Whenever I have interviewed community members and gathered data, it has consistently netted positive results.

They will also be *a powerful source for lead generation and networking*. By growing a community of passionate users and customers, you will not just be providing an environment for people to meet and get help but also a place where prospective customers can evaluate your product or service in more detail. This builds brand loyalty and often lead generation.

Now, you need to be careful here. *Do not let your sales team treat your community members as a pipeline.* This is a surefire way to annoy them. Instead, build your community and let your members naturally bring people to your business. As an example, I have sometimes set up a community concierge, where established community members can reach out to members of the company to introduce prospective customers.

Finally, *don't think of your community as merely a subservient group.* Think of them also as a group of potential mentors. As you get to know them, build friendships, and develop trust, reach out to them for guidance. Help them point you in the right direction. Help them to help you see your blind spots. This not only helps you be better at being you but it develops close relationships that will reflect well on the overall community.

IT AIN'T ALL ROSES

This all sounds pretty good, right? It is. *There is enormous opportunity wrapped up in communities, but it doesn't come for free.* It requires careful strategic design, organizational alignment, and focus. That is what this book is here to provide.

As with any initiative, there are risks attached. I don't believe in sticking your head in the sand. Instead, let's get some of these most critical risks on the table right away, and then we can design around them.

There has to be a need. Communities should be at the epicenter of where people have a shared need or interest. If you have a product or topic that no one cares about, you are going to struggle to build a community. They are not a marketing gimmick for a quick rush of interest.

Now, this doesn't mean you have to have a mass-market product or service. There are many successful niche communities, but they do need a viable audience with a potential appetite for a community.

There is no silver bullet. There simply isn't a single recipe or silver bullet for building a community. Every community is different and requires different types of attention and focus to be successful.

The method I share in this book, which I have developed over the last twenty years, is focused on how to build a *strategy* so the tactics specific to your community will naturally manifest themselves. You can think of this as a lens through which to look at communities and a blueprint in which to approach them. This will give you the foundation of how to predictably build any number of different communities.

There is no guaranteed success. I bet you didn't want to hear that one, right? There simply is no guarantee you will succeed. *"If you build it, they will come," they say. Well, they are wrong.* It should be, "If you build it, take a strategic approach, train and integrate your team tightly, carefully review results, modify your approach, and operate on a clear cadence, they will probably come." Ugh, what a mouthful, but this is how we will approach this work.

This is a cultural challenge, not a technology one. The first question some of my clients ask is, "Which technology platforms do I need to set up my community?" While this is an important consideration, it is not the first, or even fifth thing we should discuss.

Building a great community is fundamentally about creating an ecosystem in which people produce meaningful work, are able to thrive, are motivated to keep growing, and can help sustain the future success of the community. *Doing this well is all about understanding the drivers and motivations of people*, and using tech as a means to address and harness those drivers and motivations. Don't let the tech dominate your thinking.

Communities require discipline and focus. I can tell you right now that a key problem spot, which you are likely to struggle with as you start building your community, is focus. You will work through the method I present in this book, build a comprehensive strategy, and then start rolling it out. As you execute, you and your team will generate a mountain of new ideas and there will be a temptation to change course or get distracted by other things. This will become a particular challenge when you hit some of the bumps in the road with your strategy (which is perfectly normal when learning and delivering anything new).

Building a culture requires discipline and focus. It requires you and your team to show up every day to build engagement, relationships, and value. Many companies I work with struggle to stick to the plan they make, but it is important to see it through.

It will take time (and money). It takes time to put together your initial strategy, load it into a slingshot, and then launch it. It takes more time to attract people, and build clear, consistent, predictable growth and engagement.

As a general rule, building a strategy usually takes around three to six months. Building growth and participation generally takes around a year, possibly longer. Sure, there have been cases where it happens more quickly, but it depends a lot on how you approach the work, how disciplined you and your team are, and the type of community you are building.

THE BACON METHOD

When I was seven, it wasn't cool having my surname. At school my friends thought it was utterly ridiculous, and they had a point. "Your last name is a meat, you Muppet," echoed through the halls. The one benefit is that when you come up with a way of working, you can amusingly call it the Bacon Method.

To be honest, I don't actually call the approach I am sharing in this book the Bacon Method, but it is an approach that I have developed for building communities over the course of my career. I have done a lot of experimentation, have had successes and mistakes, and worked with hundreds of companies, different people, cultures, and goals.

This method is broken into ten steps that we explore throughout the book:

1. **Produce Mission and Value Statements.** First, in the next chapter we zoom out and think about the bigger picture. What is our broader mission here and what value do we want to deliver in the community—not just for our organization, but also for our prospective members?

2. **Choose Your Community Engagement Model.** Next, we choose what kind of community we want to build from

my three different models (which are also covered in chapter 2), Consumer, Champion, and Creator. This will provide a framework and some reasonable guardrails to help think about what we want to do and what our approach should be.

3. **Define What Value You Want to Deliver.** Everything has to start with *value,* and value is an equation with two critical components; the value for *you* and the value for *your members.* In chapter 3 we fill our chosen Community Engagement Model(s) with this value.

4. **Produce Your Big Rocks.** Also in chapter 3, we draft our broad objectives for the next year and ensure they have buy-in and ownership from the different stakeholders and departments in your organization. This is crucial to building a plan that the team can stick to and ensuring your team is fully aligned. Don't skip this, or heartache (and gas) lie ahead.

5. **Know Your Audience, and Build Audience Personas.** In chapter 4, we design what our target audience looks like, who they are, what value they bring, what they need to succeed, and which of these different types of audience are most critical. This will be refined into a set of audience personas, which will drive much of our further work—in particular how we find, incentivize, and engage them.

6. **Design Your On-Ramp and Engagement Model.** With our broader goals and audience clear, in chapter 5 we design the structure of our community. This covers how to build a simple and efficient onboarding

experience and how members will transition through three key phases of the community: Casual, Regular, and Core.

7. **Build Your Quarterly Plan.** With this existing strategy under our belts, the devil now rears its head in the details. We now need to break our Big Rocks down into smaller pebbles: the individual tasks that should be delivered to accomplish these big goals. This is a critical step in chapter 5 and provides the playbook for the team delivering the work.

8. **Craft Your Maturity Model and Success Criteria.** At this point, we have a firm plan in place. In chapter 7 we examine more closely what success looks like and how we can measure our progress throughout the execution of this work. We do this by using a series of maturity models and modifying them for our own needs.

9. **Execute on a Cadence.** As we execute this work, we will operate on a cadence. This involves a series of cycles, each of which has a common set of milestones and check-in meetings. This is not just a handy way of producing a manageable set of work but also a proven way of building organizational muscle and capabilities (which, as we will discuss later, is a key goal in this work).

10. **Produce Your Incentives Map.** We carefully craft a series of initiatives in chapter 8, which help transition our members through our three key community phases. This keeps people engaged and motivated, and it provides an opportunity for our future community leaders to poke their heads above the fold.

ONWARD AND UPWARD

You couldn't have picked up this book at a more exciting time. We are at this remarkable intersection in which technology, connectivity, and the social norms of a modern society pave the way for us to build powerful, engaging communities. This all provides a remarkable opportunity for businesses to provide and generate enormous value with a community.

Now, you may wonder if community members would be happy for a business to make money partially based around the contributions of all these hardworking volunteer community members. Interestingly, community members are typically happy for the financial success of businesses if they operate their community in an open, honest, and collaborative way. This is where the rubber hits the road and much of the focus of this book.

I started this first chapter with the story of Abayomi walking two hours there and back to contribute to Ubuntu. There was nothing especially unique or distinctive about why Abayomi felt that sense of devotion and commitment. It was what I saw at the time as a rather magical combination of meaning, technology, and access.

Today I understand these drivers much better, and this book will present a methodology that will fill your slingshot with the best possible material. If you are methodical, focused, and disciplined, you could be creating a community that a whole new generation of Abayomis and beyond will feel a similar sense of devotion to. Let's get to work.

CHAPTER 2

Consumers, Champions, and Collaborators

Simplicity is the ultimate sophistication.

—Leonardo da Vinci

A few years ago, an old friend asked me out one evening to help him prop up our favorite gin bar in San Francisco, Whitechapel. I could tell from the tone of his voice that this was not merely about sneaking back a few G&Ts.

"Jono, I have no idea where to begin," he blurted out with a whiff of desperation.

My friend had recently moved himself and his family to the San Francisco Bay Area having founded his new company, raised $10 million of venture funding, and now needed to build out a community around his product. This is Silicon Valley, so this was all about building growth, and building it *quickly* and *visibly*.

"I was introduced to a few community managers to figure out how this works, but they overloaded me talking about social media, blogging, events, codes of conduct, governance, forums, and a million other things. I am drowning in detail and have no idea how to tie those things to what I actually see in my head."

His problem is not unique. Almost every client I work with has the same issue. They have an instinct about how a community can provide value, but where on earth do you start?

A further thorn is that communities, and how to build them, seems enormously confusing to most people. While your hunch about the value of a community may seem clear, the reality often looks like an awkward cocktail of people, technology, and processes, all seemingly glued together in some random and unusual way.

This usually results in decision paralysis. Not only are most execs and founders new to understanding how parts of a community strategically click together but, as with my pal, when they seek help from community managers, it seems like they are speaking Greek to them, and—what's worse—answering questions they didn't ask. More confusion sets in, and that is when my phone usually rings.

"Jono, I just need a clear place to start. What are my first three steps?" This is how most of these calls begin. Then again, you probably know this—it is probably why you are reading this book in the first place.

Fortunately, there *is* a clear path and there *is* a way to make good decisions without getting bogged down in the details. Let's get started.

"MAKE A PLAN AND STICK TO IT"

I am a firm believer in intentionality. Don't *try* to do something. Don't use half measures. Get in there, roll your sleeves up, quit your excuses, and make it happen. *Results are driven not just by determination but also by a clear head and clear strategy.*

Strategy doesn't need to be complicated, but it does need to be consistent. Rod Smallwood, the manager of international rock outfit Iron Maiden, was asked how they pull off such elaborate world tours with complex live sets, carefully aligned with their recording schedule. His answer, "Make a plan and stick to it."[1]

Smallwood is right, but it isn't always quite that simple. Communities are organic, malleable, changing entities. The balance we need to strike is to *produce a strategy we are committed to delivering while being reactive to the results and regularly optimizing the strategy based on them.* In other words, "Make a plan and stick to it—and regularly make sensible updates to get better and better and better results." Sure, it is not quite as catchy, but it is critical nonetheless.

This isn't going to be a walk in the park. As Tom Hanks once memorably uttered in *A League of Their Own,* "It's supposed to be hard. If it were easy, everyone would do it."[2] If we have a clear head, shape a powerful vision, and build a realistic-yet-bold strategy, we can get quite remarkable results.

First things first: we need to zoom out. We need to get to the first principles about *why* we are doing this before we can figure out the *what* and *how.*

BUSINESS VISION AND COMMUNITY VISION: SADDLE UP

In 2014 I joined the XPRIZE Foundation as senior director of community. They are one of the most beautifully strange organizations I have ever worked with.

My new boss was the inimitable Dr. Peter Diamandis, a purveyor of boundless energy, who founded XPRIZE to run huge competitions designed to solve major problems in the world. We are not talking about building a better widget; the first XPRIZE was a $10 million competition challenging engineers of the world to build a reusable, commercially viable spacecraft back in 2004 (long before SpaceX and Virgin Galactic).

A significant reason this first XPRIZE succeeded was because Diamandis painted a powerful vision of an ambitious new age of commercial space travel, discovery, and transportation. Equally important was its clear mission: teams were challenged[3] to create a "safe, reliable, reusable, privately financed manned space ship to demonstrate that private space travel is commercially viable."

This mission was brave ("Why can't we do this?"), bold ("Why should only the government do this?"), and bullish ("Think you can do this? Prove it."). Frankly, it was nuts, but great missions (and their companion visions) are supposed to be nuts.

A community mission is different than your business vision but tightly wound around it. The vision for your business is the awesome product; the brighter future; the inspirational dream that everyone wants to get behind. The community mission is how the crowd can play a role in making your vision real.

If your business vision is to "Revolutionize how local businesses compete on the global stage," your community vision could be "To build a global community of passionate local entrepreneurs to help local business owners succeed on the global stage."

If your business vision is to "Make free legal counsel available to all members of society," your community vision could be "To build a world-class global community of legal experts focused on meaningful, citizen-focused pro-bono work."

If your business vision is to "Democratize the Internet with the most powerful cloud platform in the world," your community vision could be "To build a global community of engineers, authors, and advocates to build the most powerful and extensible cloud platform in history."

In each of these examples, the community mission provides a clear way in which the community is an engine that powers and accomplishes broader success.

Communities play a valuable role not just in delivering value for your organization but in providing a way for a broader set of people to do meaningful work. Meaning keeps people active and engaged. It generates satisfaction, a sense of belonging, and self-respect. It creates a reservoir of tribal loyalty.

This can build years of dedicated community participation. I have known community volunteers to dedicate forty hours a week of service for more than ten years because of this sense of meaning and belonging. We want this same passion and commitment in your community too. Our mission should inspire this kind of enthusiasm.

MAKE A COMMUNITY MISSION STATEMENT

Sit down with a single piece of paper and write out what you see as your community mission. Put yourself in someone else's shoes. Does it grab you?

Think carefully about how your community mission relates to your business vision. Is it clear how the community mission connects the crowd to your broader business vision?

As you work on your community mission, you may be tempted to use a second sheet of paper, start drawing complex diagrams with overlapping circles, or to break your thinking into something that looks more akin to a business plan. Resist that temptation. This isn't *War and Peace*; we don't need to overcomplicate things. Craft a few sentences and make them tight and focused.

Now get others in your organization to feed in and evolve it; their insight will be invaluable. Ask your executives, department leads, product/engineering staff, marketers, and others. Specifically ask them to challenge your thinking, find the flaws, and explore other elements you are missing. Gather their feedback, assess it, and improve your work. Remember, you want everyone to see their reflection—how they move the needle—in your community mission.

Finished with the feedback? Now take a scalpel to it. Cut the fat. Reword your community mission so it is short, memorable, and easy to rattle off at a moment's notice. Need a few examples? Head to https://www.jonobacon.com and select Resources.

KEEP YOUR MISSION
RAZOR SHARP AND IN FOCUS

I once coached a company through this exercise with their entire team in Seattle. We got an awesome business vision and community mission that the team was pumped about. A few months later I came back to the office. They had put the vision and mission in a mahogany frame and hung it next to the restroom door. People looked at it only when they were nipping out to perform their ablutions in between meetings.

Don't do this.

Your goal is to keep the business vision and community mission front and center in people's minds. Just like company values, vision and missions are like trees: they need oxygen to stay alive, grow, and thrive. They need to play a daily role in your team members' lives. They should be plastered all over the walls of your office. They should be reinforced in staff meetings and company seminars. They should be the basis of your performance reviews: did the team really have an impact on your broader business vision *and* (not *or*) your community mission? How can you integrate your business vision and community mission in the day-to-day business of your organization?

PICK A COMMUNITY
ENGAGEMENT MODEL

People often make fun of *Star Trek* for attracting particularly enthusiastic fans, but it is amusingly somewhat true. Fifty years after its debut, people are still as obsessed about the space-faring franchise as ever.

The Trek BBS is a home for many such fans.[4] This thriving online fan forum brings together more than twenty-seven-thousand Trekkies, where they discuss every element of the Starship Enterprise, Klingons, and . . . er . . . other *Star Trek* things. While twenty-seven thousand is a more-than-respectable number of members, even more astonishing is that they have together generated 6.9 million posts in these discussions.

While these are devoted fans, they are purely that—fans. They may keep demand for the *Star Trek* franchise going, which is hugely valuable, but they don't editorially contribute to or shape *Star Trek* movies, books, comic books, or video games. Fans share a common interest and often enjoy sharing it with others in communities.

Contrast this with the Ardour community, which has produced an entire open-source music production software suite.[5] Here many community members start using the program to make music, but then they discover limits to what it can do. Those who are technically inclined can create these missing features and improvements, which are then shared and integrated into the main Ardour program. In that community, members can actually shape and change the very thing that brings them together.

These and other communities differ vastly, not just because the means of participating are so different but also because the norms, expectations, culture, experience, and demands differ.

You need to think carefully about what *type* of community you want to build. Do you want something more like the Trek BBS, something more like Ardour, something in between, or something totally different?

Getting this right will help orientate your understanding and expectations about what is involved in building different communities. A little strategic feng shui if you will.

I have produced three Community Engagement Models to make this easier. You can think of each as a template or blueprint for how different types of communities work. Every community I have ever seen falls under one of these models.

Let's take a spin through them.

MODEL 1: CONSUMERS

Consumer communities are the foundation of communities just like Trek BBS that *pull together people who share a common interest.* They are relatively straightforward, with participants typically engaging in discussion around this common interest. Some may also share personal fan creations such as artwork, photography, outfits, or sculptures.

There are hundreds of thousands of these communities all around the world. They cover myriad interests from sports to fashion to movies, games, technology, and any manner of other topics.

They can be as general interest as the Reddit Science community, with its 18 million members, or as strangely specialized as athletic footwear enthusiasts in the Sneakers community, also on Reddit, with 345,000 members.[6] *Specialization is the rocket fuel that makes consumer communities fly.*

But why does this specialization work? It seems counterintuitive to our one-size-fits-all culture of generic blockbuster movies, derivative pop stars, mass-market fast food, and other things that appeal to the average of all our interests. Surely we should be more homogenized, not less?

Back in 2006, my friend Chris Anderson delved into the value of niches in his book, *The Long Tail*. In it he shared:

> The theory of the Long Tail is that our culture and economy is increasingly shifting away from a focus on a relatively small number of 'hits' (mainstream products and markets) at the head of the demand curve and toward a huge number of niches in the tail. As the costs of production and distribution fall, especially online, there is now less need to lump products and consumers into one-size-fits-all containers. In an era without the constraints of physical shelf space and other bottlenecks of distribution, narrowly targeted goods and services can be as economically attractive as mainstream fare.[7]

In other words, the Internet means that no matter how specific or strange your interest, you can find other people just like you and build content and services that serve them. Put it this way: if a video of a slightly pudgy Korean pop star dancing around riding an invisible horse can be watched 3.1 billion times on YouTube in six years and become a global phenomenon, the evidence would suggest niche interests can drum up an audience.[8]

Chris talks about niches within an economic context but his Long Tail model maps well to communities. What makes all of this tick is that human beings like to spend time with other like-minded human beings. Hang on, but isn't this surely at odds with the rather romantic notion that "opposites attract"?

Not really. Angela Bahns, associate professor of psychology at Wellesley College, and Christian Crandall, professor of social psychology at the University of Kansas, studied the nature of like-minded interactions. Spoiler alert: we are hardwired to seek out people with shared interests.

"You try to create a social world where you're comfortable, where you succeed, where you have people you can trust and with whom you can cooperate to meet your goals," Crandall says. "To create this, similarity is very useful, and people are attracted to it most of the time." Bahns adds, "We're arguing that selecting similar others as relationship partners is extremely common—so common and so widespread on so many dimensions that it could be described as a psychological default."[9]

Consumer communities are similar to an open, public clubhouse. They provide a place where people can congregate, have discussions, share ideas and opinions, showcase work they may have created, and debate different aspects of that shared interest.

In 2017, the video game industry generated $108.4 billion in revenue.[10] IGN (Imagine Games Network) has built a business serving enthusiastic fans of video games with content, communities, and more. A subsidiary of publishing powerhouse Ziff Davis, IGN is the brainchild of a different Chris Anderson, who also founded TED.

The IGN community is a Consumer model community in action. It is primarily a forum that serves as a video game clubhouse, divided into different sections based on types of games and platforms. At the time of writing there have been nearly 6 million discussions on the platform by 1.2 million members.[11] They debate the specifics of their favorite games, discuss new technologies, share maps and strategies for completing these games, discuss industry trends, and more.

Part of the simplicity of the Consumer model is that expectations of participation are very low and there is rarely any entrance criteria. Anyone is welcome to join the IGN community: you can participate as much or as little as you like. Live and let live. As such, engagement varies significantly: some people will seem wedded to the community and some will simply watch the discussions from the sidelines while munching on popcorn.

In Consumer communities, while the means *of participation is very simple, the assessment of* merit *is based on the reputation formed by showing up and taking part.* This largely mirrors how we judge others in our normal day-to-day lives at work, home, and in our relationships. How much has the person participated? How skillful are they? How respectful and polite are they? How have they helped other people, particularly weak or vulnerable people, to succeed? Did they use their turn signal when changing lanes in traffic? (Please do this, people. It drives me mad—no pun intended).

Of our three models this is by far the simplest to design and deliver results. It is also the foundation on which the others are built. More complex communities such as our Champion and Collaborator models incorporate the fundamental principles of the Consumer model.

If you want to build a community of customers and fans, this is a good model to start with.

MODEL 2:
CHAMPIONS

The Champions model, builds on top of the Consumer model and takes us a step further. Here community members go beyond discussing a shared interest to *actively delivering work that champions the success of the community and its members.* They can become an army of advocates that support the success of what you and other community members are trying to accomplish.

In the last chapter I touched on Fractal Audio Systems, who produce musical equipment, including the popular Axe-Fx line of guitar processors. They have built an impressive Champion community.

It is not merely a place of shared interest (like the Consumer model) but it has also become a place where customers go to master using the Axe-Fx, whether on the stage or in the studio.

At a simple level, the community is a discussion forum in which people ask questions and get answers. It goes further, though. There is a community wiki (a website that anyone can edit), in which pages and pages of documentation, guidance, tutorials, and reference materials have been added by volunteers across the globe. The community has also generated thousands of videos, demos, sound presets, events, and workshops.

One such community member, Alexander van Engelen, username "Yek," has written pages of documentation and guidance, and even an entire book about the Axe-Fx, all freely available. He also pours hours of his time each week into helping answer questions, provide guidance, test upcoming products, and more.

Alexander's motivations are clear: "Some people participate because they want to be part of a group. That's not my driver. I joined because I wanted to learn. The products have excellent manuals, but there was so much more information scattered around. Everybody had to search individually for answers. I took it upon myself to gather that information and wrote the 'how-tos' and book."[12]

Let's not forget: Alexander is a volunteer. He isn't on the payroll. He generates all of this value focused on the success of Fractal Audio Systems' products and users, who are a private company he doesn't actually work for. While you may not be able to fathom why on earth he would do this, thousands of people like him do.

In Champion communities, participants stroll through a progression outlined by my Product Success Model:

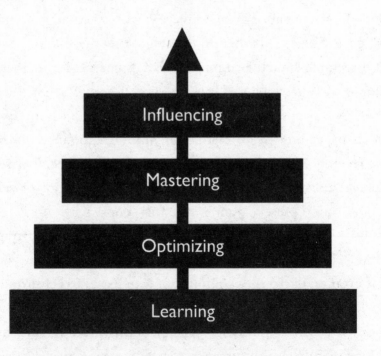

Fig. 2.1: Product Success Model

Note: This model does not cover how to "get people into the funnel" and sell people on the value of a given product or service. It presumes they are actual new customers or users. We will cover this onboarding and funnel-filling component in chapters 5 and 8.

Put yourself in a user's shoes and imagine you just purchased a new software tool for making videos. You have no idea how the darned thing works, but you have a vision of something you want to create in your head: an online video show about how to invest in the stock market like the investing guru you are.

You need to figure out how to use this tool to make this vision in your head real. You see there is a community wrapped around it, so you join.

You wade knee-deep into the first part of the Product Success Model, the Learning phase. You start asking questions, reading tutorials, and watching instructional videos in the community for how to get started. You notice that some of the same people keep answering your questions, and the place starts to feel more welcoming.

You apply the things you know and release your first stock-market video. Now you want to make your second video even better. You ask more in-depth questions and start Optimizing how you work (the second phase in the Product Success Model). Your expertise is starting to show. Other people start asking questions that you know the answer to, so you respond. You feel good about giving back, particularly as the community has been so helpful to you. You start making friends.

You learn more and are able to answer more questions. You transition into the Mastering phase. You enjoy learning and challenging yourself to make even more incredible videos, but you are also enjoying the validation and respect people in the community give you when you help them. People start referencing you more and more as a "rock star" (if only they knew . . .). It feels good; the community is fun, rewarding, and you are getting a lot out of it.

This personal validation gives you even more of an inclination to give back. You start producing new videos about using the software itself. People love them. So you start a blog where you share more ideas. When other community members come to your local town, you meet them for drinks. You are Influencing and a fully formed champion. You and "Yek" should probably hang out.

This is a powerful model for generating multiple value streams: support, content, relationships, and advocacy. While it is a heavier lift, it can work well for products and services where there is a genuine passion and utility.

MODEL 3: COLLABORATORS

The Collaborators model takes the content-creation aspect of the Champion model, bolts on a jetpack, and presses a big glowing Launch button. Remember when we talked about how people in the Ardour music production suite community would add features to the program itself? That is a Collaborator community.

Here enthusiastic participants don't just add independent pieces of work to the stockpile; they *actively work together as a team on shared projects*. This can unlock some quite literally world-changing opportunity.

On June 7, 2014, a new open-source project called Kubernetes was announced. It was a piece of software that could be used for managing how software services run on the cloud. I won't bore you too much with what Kubernetes does, but safe to say, it rocked the tech and enterprise world.

A critical element of why Kubernetes succeeded is that it is open-source. This means that its code is freely available and when there are gaps in functionality, or bugs that cause problems for users, there is a way in which anyone (who meets certain guidelines) can fill in these gaps and create these additional features or fixes. Importantly, once someone creates a missing feature, it is shared with everyone.

Four years later, more than two thousand developers have contributed improvements to the project, shipping more than 480 releases.[13] These developers come from more than fifty companies (many of whom compete with one another) as well as independent volunteers. Welcome to the Collaborator community model in action.

What is neat about this model is that the value of Kubernetes (as one such example) increases as more people roll their sleeves up and get involved. If you spend one hour of your time contributing an improvement to the project and ten other people do the same, your one-hour investment will net ten additional hours of value from other people.

As your community grows, it often offers greater and greater added value. This is one of the major reasons why open source has succeeded and now powers the Internet, businesses, the devices in your home, the electrical grid, and beyond: the community is a fundamental part of the value proposition, arguably as important as the software itself.

Of course, there will always be users who consume the fruits of a community but don't contribute back ("freeloaders," as grumpy cynics may say before their morning coffee). This is totally fine though. If your Collaborator community always grows and keeps generating new contributions, everyone involved, freeloaders included, will experience continued—and often significant—benefits.

Interestingly, much like stifled yawns around a boardroom table, collaboration can be infectious. When people work together out in the open, solving common, tangible problems, it generates social capital and respect, and onlookers often want to get in on the action. Sometimes the freeloaders are inspired to contribute too!

When this happens, it creates something psychologists call a *diffusion chain*, in which people basically mimic the behavior of others.[14] This act of mimicking strangely results in people often getting better results more quickly, as there is an intrinsic social desire to be accepted like the person the individual is mimicking.

Collaborator communities need to be wired up carefully so people can contribute and collaborate effectively with others. Decisions need to be made quickly and objectively, and there needs to be a fair playing field for everyone involved. To accomplish this we need to mix together four key ingredients in our Collaborator petri dish.

First, *provide clear, open access for collaboration.* Everyone needs to be on the same playing field and have access to the same tools, guidance, and other facilities. You can't build a team unless the team has the same tools and opportunity. If some people can access certain tools and others can't, you will have problems. The bedrock of these kinds of communities is asynchronous access; you can access any of these tools and facilities from anywhere at any time. This access should be as unlimited and unencumbered as possible.

Second, *create a simple and clear peer-review process.* This should help you determine quality based on the merit of the individual contribution. There needs to be a way in which anyone can contribute something new but their work is vetted for quality, irrespective of who they are or where they come from. This should be simple, clear, and effective.

Third, *your collaborative workflow should be open to change.* Just as your desk at work is set up exactly as you like it so you can be comfortable and efficient, your contributors want the same. Don't create an immutable, solid workflow that never changes. Let the community help to fine-tune and improve how they work together.

The fourth component, and a critical one, is to *provide equal opportunity and a level playing field.* Everyone needs to have an opportunity to shine. I don't just mean that we clearly welcome everyone irrespective of gender, color, sexuality, socioeconomic background, or other factors but also that everyone can deliver work that is judged objectively for merit.

This is often described as *meritocracy,* but be careful. Meritocracy is not a framework that can be followed to get predictable, objective results. It is a North Star, a philosophy, and a value that we should strive for.

I am sure some of you are thinking, "Hold your horses there, Bacon. If I am running a business and building a community around it, surely I shouldn't be an equal. I should be in a position of authority. Shouldn't I be in charge?"

Yes and no. As great leaders repeatedly demonstrate, building productive, effective organizations and teams isn't about putting people into boxes of "managers" and "subordinates." *It is about building a culture where everyone is empowered to be their best.*

I used to work with a guy called Colin. He was an engineer. He wasn't a manger or a particularly visible employee. He was quiet, a little conservative, but a diligent and talented worker. He treated people as equals with courtesy and respect, and he delivered amazing work. While the company had a hierarchy and reporting line, great work could bubble up from anyone, and Colin was seen as a central figure. He developed remarkable respect from his peers, arguably more than some members of the leadership team. The environment supported his success. Great Collaborator communities do the same.

Collaborator communities are by far the most complex of our three models, but they can offer enormous benefits when well run. Many organizations have built successful businesses and global brands based around these kinds of communities, especially in the technology sector. These include our earlier examples of companies such as Docker and Red Hat, with the former valued at $1.3 billion and the latter—at the time of writing having sixty-two straight quarters of revenue growth—with an annual revenue of more than $3 billion.[15] The core of their businesses are intentional, open, meritocratic communities; done well, the sky is the limit.

DIGGING DEEPER:
INNER OR OUTER COLLABORATION

Before we go on, I want to touch on an important subtlety in Collaborator communities. They actually come in two great-tasting flavors. I call them Inner and Outer.

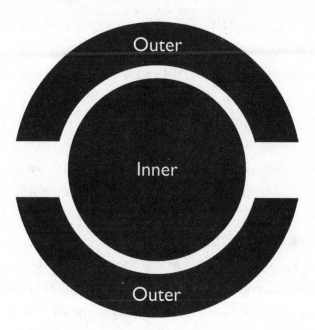

Fig. 2.2: Inner and Outer Collaborator Communities

In the majority of open-source communities that I have worked with, people participate in the same core product the company works on. They add code, documentation, translations, and more.

An example of this is TensorFlow. Originally started by Google in 2015, this open-source, machine-learning project has attracted more than seventeen hundred contributors.[16] Not only is the code open, but discussion of the project, working groups that define direction and focus, and issue and bug reports are all open too. This has resulted in TensorFlow being used by companies such as Coca-Cola, Airbnb, Swisscom, Intel, PayPal, Twitter, Lenovo, and many others.[17]

Their success and ability to solicit so many contributions would be significantly reduced without such a strong community backbone and an environment where everyone plays on the same playing field. Although volunteers, they are effectively members of the team, and as such expect to be treated as members of the team. They care deeply about how decisions are made (such as in the working groups in the TensorFlow example), how people work together, when and where meetings are held, how trademarks can be used by the community, how the community is governed, and other related topics. I call these Inner types of community.

Contrast this with Apple's and Google's mobile platforms. App developers build on top of those platforms. They care deeply that the platform works, has great resources for how to use it, and gets exposure for their apps in the broader market. Because they consume the platform, they don't feel as much ownership over how it is created; they mainly care that they can use it. This is an Outer type of community.

Speaking of which, *ownership is a key distinction between Inner and Outer communities*. In an Inner community the member feels a shared sense of responsibility and ownership in the project (hence wanting to be treated as a team member). In an Outer community members feel ownership of their app/product but not of the platform they are building it on. Think carefully about this relationship with ownership and how it affects your community.

Unsurprisingly, the care and feeding of these communities requires quite different approaches. The Inner needs to be carefully managed to create a team environment where *everyone is treated equally in how they collaborate and work*. Reduce the gaps between your staff and community members as best you can. You can never make everyone completely equal, as there will be certain business dynamics that make this more complicated (confidential contracts, security issues, etc.), but this is another North Star to aim for.

The Outer is about delivering a world-class platform that gets people up and running quickly and easily and where *they are taken care of as content creators.* Your primary goal should be an end-to-end experience with all the different pieces available and within easy reach.

CREATE A PEOPLE-POWERED MARKETING MACHINE

Unsurprisingly, all of these models have a remarkable domino effect on the marketing and awareness of your product or service.

When Ubuntu was started in 2004, it gained initial traction. Then I joined in 2006 and started building out the community. While Ubuntu was a technology project, I didn't want to merely attract the code-writing neckbeards. I wanted to be more ambitious and encourage different types of contributions, from engineering to support to documentation, as well as advocacy, events, and translations.

This diversity of participation, and therefore content, had a tangible brand impact. As one data point with the following Google Trends graph shows, as the community started kicking into gear, the word "Ubuntu" became more prominently searched for and surfaced in more searches.

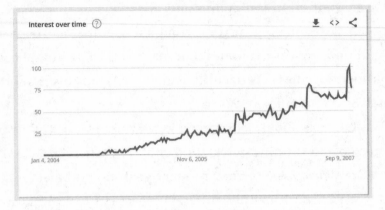

Fig. 2.3: The growth of people searching for Ubuntu on Google.[18]

As the community produced more content and support, it broadened the surface area of material, which helped pull more people in from the outside. The brand was getting stronger.

This didn't just widen Ubuntu's reach and brand exposure; it also increased the value of the community itself. In addition to higher search rankings, our community experienced increased traffic, usage, and growth, which in turn generated more value.

Momentum builds momentum. Humans are attracted to things that clearly add value to other humans. Similarly, great service and experiences inspire people to encourage their friends to experience the same. This generates a *referral halo.*

An example of this is the tile installer who worked on our recent remodel. Danny doesn't care about having a website or social media presence for his business, and he performs zero advertising. His entire business is fueled by referrals from his excellent work. This works because (a) we often want people who deliver great products and experiences to enjoy continued success, and (b) if we can have our friends enjoy this experience, it puts us in a favorable social position in the eyes of both our friends and the provider of the product/experience.

Now, this referral halo doesn't just cover the individual experience but also group experiences. If you and a friend are walking down a street on a Saturday night, and you poke your nose into a restaurant where everyone is smiling and having a great time, and there is a table free, you will probably go in. Good experiences, particularly in groups, are infectious. This is how we build growth.

Now, we need to be realistic. If the restauranteur focuses only on good food and not on getting bums on seats, they will still have an empty restaurant. As such, you need to focus on building both *meaningful value* and *driving consumption of it*. This will help you to really harness this momentum effect.

HOW TO PICK THE RIGHT COMMUNITY ENGAGEMENT MODEL FOR YOU

OK, enough talk about the models. Let's now zone in on which ones work best for you.

It will come as no surprise that there is no one-size-fits-all solution here. I wish there was, as it would make my job infinitely easier (and cause less heartburn). For some of you, there will be a clear fit, but for others you may have a blend of multiple models in the same community. Blending multiple models is perfectly normal, certainly for larger communities. Either way, great communities start simple and then iterate and evolve.

A few months back I wrapped up an engagement with a company who had started a community the year prior. They initially wanted to go all-in guns blazing. They wanted people to provide support and guidance, provide feature feedback, produce art, deliver events, moderate and maintain forums, provide mentoring and more. In the wise words of AC/DC's Bon Scott, it was a "touch too much."[19]

Don't do this.

Start simple, pick one model, and get cracking. Build your community based on the guidance I provide throughout this book and when you start seeing sustainable results, expand into other areas. You need to learn to walk before you run and then ultimately sprint.

Why? Two reasons. First, if you overcomplicate your first chunk of community strategy, it can become an unwieldy, wiry mess that is difficult to untangle if you get stuck or overwhelmed. This can be a huge headache, so starting simple reduces this complexity.

Second, the only way to learn this stuff is to roll your sleeves up and get to work. As you are new at this, *starting simple gives you and your team time to learn and grow.* Don't overwhelm everyone with too large a plate of things to do. You will get better results if you have time to understand this work, digest how it is received, and be thoughtful in how you improve.

Let's look at some common scenarios and which models are a good fit. This should give you a general sense of what kind of ingredients you will want to include. *How* we add those ingredients will be covered throughout the rest of the book.

Scenario 1: I want to build a community . . . where people are fans and users of my product or service.

Use a Consumer model.

Commonly this is delivered as a public discussion forum or channel where people can join, browse previous discussions, share their ideas and opinions, ask questions, and otherwise consumer-related material. This would be similar to our earlier TrekBBS example. You provide a simple, easy-to-navigate, virtual clubhouse for people to have discussions on a range of topics that relate to your product or service.

These kinds of communities are discussion- and content-driven with preproduced material (primarily coming from you) such as articles and videos, as well as targeted discussions. Plan to (a) provide an environment where people can have these discussions, and (b) produce content that will constantly pull people in, such as news, updates, events, and videos. This will keep people coming back for more, and when they do come back you should be engaging, inspirational, and encouraging.

Scenario 2: I want to build a community . . . where people provide help and support.

Use a Champion model.

This can apply to both an official community for a product or service, or an enthusiast-driven, unofficial community. On one hand, you need to provide a place where people can ask and answer questions but where you can also ensure previous questions and answers can be easily found. This then increases the reusable value of those solutions. The more we can reuse content, the greater value it offers. Fortunately, there are lots of ways to do this.

As an example, the Seasoned Advice community provides a place where people can post questions about all manner of different cooking, baking, grilling, and other culinary interests.[20] Questions can be submitted, multiple answers are provided by the community, and then the question-submitter picks the right answer. These question-answer combinations provide an incredible archive of reusable questions, making it into a huge FAQ for cooking (and often these questions and answers pop up when people search on Google too!). There are similar communities for mathematics, music theory, homebrewing, and many more.[21]

You will also need to enable the community to produce precanned material and resources such as tutorials, videos, and online courses. Your members will need to be able to not just create this material but also publish it where other people can find it.

You will also want to ensure that you recognize and reward people who provide great support and produce great content. This will keep them coming back and build a sense of belonging (similar to our stock market video project example earlier).

Scenario 3: I want to build a community . . . where people create technology that runs on my platform.

This is the Collaborator model, but as we discussed earlier, it will be of the Outer type.

Your number one goal here is to provide a world-class experience in how new participants can get up and running building their technology on top of your platform. This experience needs to be simple, intuitive, and cover the varying needs of your audience. These developers could use any platform, so presume they have limited patience—get them delivering great results as quickly and easily as possible. As we cover later in chapter 5, it is critical that we test our on-ramps to ensure that they, y'know, actually work.

Simplifying the onboarding of new members requires two key areas of focus.

First, *make building on your platform as simple as possible,* such as ensuring you have a solid developer kit, documentation, and a place where members can ask questions and get help. Google does a good job here with their Android developer platform.[22] They provide a downloadable Software Development Kit (SDK), code samples, testing/quality guidelines, and a library of documentation.

Developers should see results within a short period of time (such as thirty minutes). Ensure the onboarding experience is tight and focused. We will delve into onboarding in more detail in chapter 5.

Second, *have a plan to incentivize developers* to promote and raise awareness of their applications and working with your platform. Their testimonials of your platform are a good hook to bring other developers in.

Scenario 4: I want to build a community . . . where people create functionality and improvements to my product or service.

Use the Collaborator model and the Inner type within it.

Your core goal here is to create a great team environment for both your staff and community members. The more open you are, and the fewer differences between staff and community members, the easier the community will be to build. Everyone will get on and live in (mostly) perfect harmony.

Our earlier mentions of Ardour and Kubernetes are good examples of this. They provide clear, open collaboration and development. Many other projects, such as Discourse and Fedora, are similarly good examples.[23]

People need a way to understand what they can do to help, how to submit contributions and have them peer reviewed, where to get help when they need it, how to be involved in reasonable levels of planning and coordination, and other elements. If your staff are able to do this well and out in the open, you will already have a great starting point.

You will also need a clear leadership-and-governance methodology; this is commonplace in similar communities. It doesn't mean you hand over the reins to the community, but you involve them in leadership where it makes sense (and where they have earned a place at the table). The leadership element is one of the most delicate balances to strike, and we will discuss it throughout this book. It is just like running a business: you want to ensure people feel invested and autonomous.

Scenario 5: I want to build a community . . . inside my company to optimize how people and teams work together.

Internal communities (often as part of digital transformation initiatives) can take a few different approaches. If your primary goal is educating staff to work more effectively and share approaches to solving problems, you should use the Champion model as discussed in scenario 2, but it would obviously be explicitly focused on an internal audience.

If your primary goal is encouraging different teams to collaborate together on shared projects, this will be a Collaborator model (the Inner type), similar in scope to scenario 4.

Ensure you take an extra level of care and attention in matching your community to the corporate culture and obtaining approvals from managers to have their teams participate. A financial services client I worked with on a digital transformation project had great results within a tightly insulated team, but he struggled to broaden out the initiative until all the necessary managers were on board. This required a lot of political maneuvering to build support, but then the work and results flowed much more freely.

You need to treat your internal community as volunteer in nature. *Differentiate between requirements and requests.* Some companies see an internal community member do good work and then load them up with extra work they *have* to do. This produces the opposite of your desired effect and can make people reluctant to join.

SIX FOUNDATIONAL KEY PRINCIPLES AND HOW TO APPLY THEM (AND NOT SCREW THEM UP)

At this point in our journey we are laying our foundations. Each Community Engagement Model provides a mold in which we pour a mixture of other ingredients that will help our community to grow.

Before we move on, there are six important principles you should follow, irrespective of which model(s) you are using and what kind of community you are building. Think of these as a tonic for keeping your foundation strong and healthy.

1. Start Simple and Build Valuable Assets

When an unknown filmmaker makes their first movie, it has value to them but it is largely worthless to other people. There are no fans, there is no platform. There is one asset, the film, that is unproven in the broader marketplace.

Communities are the same. Your brand-new community infrastructure and facilities will be unused, your new social accounts will have no followers, and your events will have no RSVPs. We have to start somewhere, and right out of the gate things are pretty barren.

When you build a new community, *limit the number of moving pieces.* Keep things simple, start small, and build up. Pick a few key components and build significant value around them. Expand later.

One community I inherited originally spent months putting together all manner of tools: a website, blog, six social accounts, wiki, mailing list, and more. If this wasn't overkill, I don't know what is. They spent more time discussing how these tools worked than actually doing anything that was constructive. What a waste of time and effort.

Start with a Minimum (read that word again) Viable Product, to provide just enough infrastructure and workflow to allow your members to generate value. Where possible, pick single solutions: one social network, one forum, one collaboration tool. Generate value, and then expand from there.

2. Have Clear and Objective Leadership

There is a cliché about people being either leaders or followers, but it is largely true. What's more, there are a darn sight more followers than leaders in the world. Your community is going to need clear, decisive, and fair leadership. This will not just help you be successful; importantly, others will be guided by this leadership, often emulating it, and you want this to be driven by the *right* behavioral patterns and leadership.

This leadership needs to be clear, intentional, approachable, and objective. How you do this depends on your community. It could vary from a single leader right up to a complex set of leadership teams that represent different parts of the community. Again, start small and evolve.

Your leadership needs to be focused but approachable. Mårten Mickos is CEO of HackerOne, a security company in San Francisco. He has put their community of security researchers front and center in how they have built their business, and subsequently value, in the market.

A few years back HackerOne invited some of their most accomplished community members to a lavish-yet-intimate security event in Las Vegas. Mårten made it clear he was in service of their success. He wanted to learn their motivations, interests, and how he could help them; he was passionate about learning from them how he could be a better leader. He even fetched them drinks and snacks while they feverishly worked.

Like Mårten, great leaders listen, learn, and guide. They don't dominate, keep people down, or control unnecessarily. A great leader is clear in the scope of their leadership and intentions, open and transparent in their actions, but can be private and nuanced when required. A great leader can help your community members to make decisions, resolve conflict, and always provide a calm, steady hand. Think carefully who you can put in place who possesses these attributes.

3. Clear Culture and Expectations

My wife and I know a couple who for years have argued like cats and dogs. While all marriages can get testy when kids, tiredness, and stress are mixed in, their Achilles heel has always been unclear expectations. "You were supposed to pick the kids up!" "You didn't tell me I needed to be at the school at that time!"

This problem gets exponentially worse as you chuck more people into the mixing bowl. *When people get together, culture forms.* Within that culture are social norms that are expected to be adhered to but are largely unspoken. As the group grows, there can be a divergence of what these norms can and should be, which cause a significant amount of the interpersonal problems in communities and businesses.

It is essential to *always set clear expectations and cultural norms in a community.* There should be no ambiguity about your values and the social fabric of how the community operates. If you think everyone understands this, they probably don't. You need to define this and *constantly* remind people of these values on a day-to-day basis.

This isn't hard: it can be as simple as creating a document with a clear set of values that the community will always adhere to. I often recommend to clients that they create a Community Promise, which contains their core values that may be obvious to us but are important to boldly state. This often includes elements such as:

- We criticize ideas, not people.
- We treat people as equals and everyone is welcome in our community, irrespective of their gender, sexuality, political orientation, or otherwise.
- We judge contributions based on their individual merit.
- The vast majority of collaboration in our community happens openly, with limited exceptions for security or customer reasons.
- We believe in "fail forward." We don't demonize people for failure but embrace it to learn and improve.

Documents like this can clarify general principles and values, but it is critical not just that you enforce them (and be *seen* enforcing them) but also that there is a regular flow of information and updates to underline how the documents are in place and thriving. Remember: *a critical part of the community "product" is a healthy, inclusive, engaging culture*: you need to market and maintain that culture to keep it thriving. This culture has to be a malleable entity that everyone can positively influence.

I worked with a large financial services client in London last year. Over lunch an employee was bemoaning the indignity of spending every day in a cube, unable to influence the culture of the business. *Influence is psychologically important to us*, not just to validate our own work, but to build a sense of belonging in a group.

Focus on building a culture with clear expectations but one that is "hackable." Regularly gather community feedback, learn from it, and refine standards of practice and workflow. *Culture is evolved by its participants, not an unchangeable rulebook handed down by the gods.*

4. Focus on Relationships, Trust, and Engagement

Life is all about relationships and trust. From our families, to workplaces, to friends: if you don't cherish and build relationships, you are doing it all wrong. Also, your friends will think you suck.

Trust is the connective tissue in a relationship. You need to create an environment that doesn't just solve problems but fosters relationships that can grow trust. This will build a skeleton on which everything else will flourish.

Your approach to this will significantly influence the success of your community. Don't see your community members and teams as pure utility and function; they should be a network of relationships that form a strong human foundation in your community. It is these relationships that will reduce the dependency on your initial guidance and mentorship, and give community members the confidence to innovate and build new value in the community. It is critical you build this autonomy in your members; it is how you grow.

It is simple, really: invest yourself in other people's success, be interested in their story, and treat them like equals. From there a healthy culture can form.

5. Strive for and Be Reactive to Insight

I am going to annoy a lot of product managers right now.

There is an arrogance in the halls of many businesses that the people sitting around the conference room table have all the answers. Elegantly drawn diagrams on whiteboards, oft-referenced TED talks and books, and other evidence tries to solidify their case.

Here's the thing: when you build anything for people, including products, services, or communities, *the answers to your questions live in the heads of your audience.* We just need to tease them out in a form that we can act on.

Throughout this process of building a community you are going to have a lot of questions. As your experience grows, it can be tempting to think you know what the answers are, but you probably have a hunch at best. Your audience is the true source of wisdom, but they may not know it. Ask them questions, probe theories, and make yourself vulnerable to constructive criticism. It will benefit you significantly.

As part of this process, *you have to be open to uncomfortable insight. You are going to screw up.* Be stoic in the face of difficult-to-swallow feedback. Critical feedback is a *good* thing: it shines a light on a leaky hole in our sailboat. Doing this well not only plugs the hole but it builds remarkable trust with our community, trust that is often shared with others.

6. Be Surprising

Finally, the very best companies and communities always surprise their audiences (in a good way).

Ted Cruz, a prominent conservative politician, was once a guest on *The Late Show with Stephen Colbert,* where he shared his opposition to a Supreme Court ruling on gay marriage.[24] When the audience booed him, Colbert responded with "Guys, guys, however you feel, he's my guest, so please don't boo him." Colbert, while a clear supporter of gay rights, surprised his audience. He felt it important to provide his guests with the ability to share their views unencumbered, even if he and others disagreed with them.

People need to be surprised, inspired, and challenged. This is not about being a cheap provocateur, but instead about always delighting your members and team with your ability to push new boundaries and enforce critical values. My example of Mårten Mickos earlier demonstrates this. Watching such an accomplished CEO take an interest in learning from his community (and grabbing them drinks), really stuck with people. It bucked the trend of how many people saw CEOs.

This is not just a key leadership skill. It will ward off stagnation and boredom as your community ages. *Keep them on their toes.* The right kinds of positive surprises will continue to build faith in your community's ability to accomplish its mission, faith in you, and subsequently, faith in your vision.

TOWARD VALUE:
ALL KILLER, NO FILLER

Jim Zemlin is the executive director of the Linux Foundation, an organization that facilitates hundreds of technology communities across the cloud, infrastructure, automobile, data, and beyond. In a recent discussion I had with him he touched on an important component of delivering this broader strategy, "A mistake some companies make is an unwillingness to give up any control."

He continues, "This manifests in different ways, ranging from the community's governance, funding, the identity of the main-tainers (and whether there is a growth path for outside con-tributors), the openness of the project, transparency of decision making, and more. Companies must be willing to release some control of the project to the community, or they risk ending up with a pseudo-open project."[25]

As we have covered so far, the *authenticity* of your community is critical. Key to that authenticity is building a collaborative environment where your community is empowered to do great work. For this to thrive you need to think carefully about this balance of power between your company and the community.

As Jim says, "Companies can still be leaders of the project without the tight control checks typically exercised in internal projects."[26] He isn't wrong. The true test of your community strategy is not making people jump through hoops to approve their work, but instead making them *want* to jump through hoops to help them, you, and the rest of the community be successful.

CHAPTER 3

Build It and They (May) Come

The world needs new leadership, but the new leadership is about working together.

—Jack Ma

"Hello, Jono. How was your weekend?" asked Don, an affable and always-eager member of a community I used to run. (For the sake of this story, Don has been anonymized; he definitely looks more like a "Dave.")

"Good, thanks!" I said. "How was the event you organized this weekend? Did you get a good turnout?"

There was an audible lump in Don's throat. "Er, not great. No one showed up."

I nervously giggled. Don, somewhat awkwardly, didn't repay the favor.

He wasn't lying. He organized an event, booked the room, coordinated the content, organized the coffee and snacks, and no one came. Not a sausage. He built it and they didn't actually come. Heck, it almost seemed they avoided the damn place.

While Don could laugh it off, there is a lesson in all of this. The reason people didn't attend was because it wasn't clear what *value* the event offered to them. Don didn't connect his scheduled content and networking to the benefits attendees could receive from the overall experience (e.g., knowledge and relationships).

It doesn't matter if he put together the venue, coffee, seating, and advertising. Knowing and mixing in these ingredients is simply not enough. They are a baseline.

This is where many companies new to community strategy get stuck. They hire a community manager, and that person starts mixing in the different ingredients we expect to see such as social media, blogging, events, and marketing. There is a risk here though: *if you are not clear in what* value *your audience wants and how you can deliver it* quickly and reliably *for them, you risk a lot of work and a lot of failure.*

UNPICKING VALUE

Value is simply defined as something of "relative worth, utility, or importance."[1] It comes in two great-tasting flavors.

Tangible value refers to measurable, physical goods and services you can see, touch, and feel. It is the salary you get at work, the free travel you get with your airline rewards program, the complimentary coffee you get when your tenth stamp is added to your coffee rewards card.

Intangible value are the benefits you experience and feel. It is being Employee of the Month, the thrill of working with smart people, being appreciated for your work, seeing your work being used and valued by others, and feeling part of a team you care about.

Psychologically, we humans are wired up to be quite willing to invest our time and effort if there is an outcome we consider valuable. This is why we have jobs, take part in competitions, and work our socks off to get into new professional positions, desired colleges, and other things we want. If we can (a) clearly see how we can *contribute* value, and (b) clearly see how we can *receive* value, we have the foundation for a great community.

This gives us our next step: to *crisply understand what tangible* and *intangible value we should generate in our communities.* This gets us thinking in the right way and also provides guardrails to ensure the nitty-gritty strategic and tactical details we craft later always have a dotted line to the most important focus of our work: driving *value.*

Danger, Will Robinson! The mistake many organizations make when thinking about value is to become naval-gazing, selfish teenagers. *What can* my *organization get out of the community? What can these community members do for* us*? How can it help* our *business?* This is a fast track to a boring community.

Successful relationships, whether they are marriages, partnerships, friendships, etc., are all about understanding what makes the other person tick, and how you can make them happy. *The role of empathy and selflessness has proven time and time again to both build relationships and repair them.* It is the bedrock of great leadership throughout the ages.

If we can understand and articulate the value we can generate for both our future community members and ourselves, we can build a community that is exciting for them and worthwhile for us. Let's get started.

CREATE A VALUE STATEMENT

Grab a piece of paper and a pencil. We are going into brain-storming mode. Divide the paper in half and start jotting down what kind of value you see for your organization and for your members, just like in figure 3.1.

Value I want to build for...	
My Organization	**Community Members**
•	•
•	•
•	•
•	•

Fig. 3.1: Community Value Statement

What you choose to focus on here will be largely based on your Community Mission Statement (from chapter 2) and which Community Engagement Model(s) you have chosen.

Value for the Community Member

Here is rule number one for how to build great communities: *put the success and value of your prospective members first.* If you get that right, success for your organization will naturally flow.

Sketch out the value for your community members first. Not only will this give you a clear idea of how to produce a genuinely valuable and interesting community, it will also calibrate your expectations for how much you can realistically commit to shaping this value for your members.

Put yourself in the shoes of prospective members. You are potentially interested in joining the community, but you have little time and a million other distractions to take your attention away. What are the things you care about most? What are the most immediate problems you want to solve? What would be the ideal experience that delivers personal value to you?

We all evaluate new things first as window shoppers. Before you buy that new tool for your business, you search online to understand what it can do. Before you buy a product, you read the reviews. Before you fix your bathroom sink pipe, you browse online for how to do it.

We do the same with communities. If a community is open to browse (such as a public forum), many prospective community members may never sign up for your community but will actively consume the fruits of it. For example, I have been learning about music production for years from the HomeRecording.com community. I can read it openly, but I have barely contributed.

Of course, many people do want to dig deeper. They need information, guidance, and answers to their specific questions. They want to work with others on a shared project. They want to contribute new content. These are *all* opportunities for the community to work together to produce value for themselves and others.

Now, be realistic. Don't assume a community member's primary or even secondary priority is that you and your organization are successful. Don't assume they have bags of time. *What value can they consume that is objectively good for them and them only?* Let's look at some common areas of value we see in different communities.

1. *Meeting Other (Awesome) People.* Don't underestimate the value of simply meeting other people like you. Discussing a shared interest, sharing ideas, having debates, and making new friends can be hugely rewarding.

2. *Interesting Content That Enriches Their Experience.* Communities can be a powerful engine for content. Great content can be videos, articles, podcasts, live events, images, source material (e.g., editable 3D objects), items inside digital environments (such as objects and buildings), and more.

This value should be two-fold: *consuming* all this great content but also *producing* content and enjoying other people enjoying it for themselves.

3. *High-Quality Education and Getting Help.* A common first entry-point for new community members is finding help to solve their problems, particularly when picking up a new product or service. This typically comes in two forms: educational material such as guides and tutorials that provide guidance for solving problems, and answers from human beings available to troubleshoot with. This is a major area of value and consistently successful in communities.

4. *Skills Development.* Communities are a fantastic way for people to "cut their teeth" and refine their skills. They provide an environment where you can produce something, such as writing, design, or software, and then others can provide feedback and help you refine your skills. This is often done in an open setting, which also builds confidence and capabilities.

5. *Mentoring and Coaching.* Across the world there are millions of kind souls who provide guidance, mentoring, and advice to their fellow community members. This can offer significant value. Think about it: you can join a community, have access to smart, talented

people who can provide invaluable mentoring, and it doesn't cost the community member a dime. Make this a key selling point.

6. *Career Experience and Expertise.* If your community is professional in nature, such as an internal community in your company or a community focused on professional products and services, this is an important consideration. Communities can provide a great way to build experience and even start putting together additions to a résumé. I wouldn't be writing this book if it were not for the experiences, people, and opportunities that I gleaned from participating in communities.

Updating Your Community Value Statement

As you consider these different areas of value for your members, remember we are not merely building a vending machine where you put effort in and get value out. We want to make the experience personal and drive intangible human value too.

This is a community. Our members should be able to create lasting relationships, be appreciated and validated for their contributions, feel a part of the broader success of the community, and develop an authentic sense of belonging. *People are initially attracted to communities for the tangible value, but the intangible value keeps them coming back for more.*

Here are some examples of items for your Community Value Statement:

- I want community members to be able to ask questions and get knowledgeable, reliable answers within twenty-four hours.

- I want community members to be able to produce and share best practice, guidance, and documentation, and enjoy it being used by others.
- I want community members to produce applications and services that support the broader success of our community.
- I want community members to be able to contribute features to our software and see their features used and appreciated.
- I want community members to be able to have free, open access to our product.
- I want community members to learn new skills and develop valuable experience for their career.
- I want community members to have fun and enjoy their time in the community.

That last one is critical. *Communities need to be fun!* Your members want to have a good time. They want to do interesting work, have fun and engaging discussions, and build relationships. They don't want a dry, boring, mechanical, overly formal experience. If you are unsure what *fun* means to your prospective members, look at similar successful communities for how they make it fun and engaging.

Value for Your Organization

As I have already mentioned, communities are no walk in the park for organizations to set up. They require investment, time, and consistent nurturing. While they offer tremendous opportunities, you should be clear in what *you* want to accomplish.

This is particularly important in building buy-in. The vast majority of my clients kick off their community strategy with a group of enthusiastic, energetic, stakeholders and sponsors. They then need to sell their vision to other teams to get them onboard to play a role in making it actually happen. Unless the value of this work is clear and unambiguous, other teams will find reasons to pass the buck, ignore it, or roll their eyes when the topic of work assignments pops up. *We don't just want their buy-in; we want their enthusiasm, passion, and expertise.*

Let's look at some common areas of value many organizations are looking for when they build out their community programs. These should sell both the passionate and dispassionate on why this community will be worth the time and effort.

1. *Customer and User Growth.* Potential customers often use a community to evaluate a product by seeing how other people use it, asking questions about how it could work for them, and knowing they have a place they can get help. Communities can also play an enormous role in advocating your product or service with others.

2. *Better Support for Customers and/or Users.* On the other side of the equation, communities can provide fantastic free support for your product. They can answer questions, troubleshoot problems, and provide guidance for how they can get the most value out of using it.

3. *Improved Marketing and Brand Recognition.* Communities can be an army for brand builders. They can raise awareness, produce content, share material on social media, speak at conferences, organize user groups, advocate for you in their businesses, and more.

4. *Technology/Product Production and Enhancement.* Many communities, particularly those using the Collaborator Community Participation Model, can generate hugely valuable technology contributions.

For Inner Collaborator communities this can be producing new features, fixing bugs and security issues, improving translations, and improving infrastructure. For Outer Collaborator communities this can be building applications, integrations, services, and more. All of this makes your platform or product more powerful.

5. *Recruiting and Services.* When you have a passionate, enthusiastic community wrapped around your product or service, they can be a good source of potential hires for your company. It makes sense: they have the domain experience and expertise, and they can be a set of highly qualified leads to fill various roles.

Also, you can transform this expertise into consulting and partner relationships where you can have key community members provide training, support, and other services. This all broadens out the ecosystem.

As you think about the value you want to build for your organization, you have to be realistic with what resources you have available and how much you can do, but also what makes sense for you strategically. Communities with a commercial backer or stakeholder need a careful balance, or disaster can rear its ugly head. You need to focus on value that is compatible with the interests of your community members. Otherwise you will create a community that people couldn't care less about.

For example, most members would be happy to produce content, material, or technology that adds value to the broader community (e.g., help for other users), but they are unlikely to produce material that is only going to benefit you and your business (e.g., providing support as part of your paid support service). This is a consistent pattern I see: *community members want to serve the community, of which your organization is one cog in the machine.*

Similarly, the value you drive shouldn't be "cheap." I have worked with many SVPs of Sales and Marketing who initially cackle in excitement thinking of this pool of people to spam with sales material.

Don't do this.

Think of your community as a trusted partner; would you spam a trusted partner? No. Would you want to harness that partner for your organization in a way they are comfortable with? Sure.

Updating Your Community Value Statement

Here are some examples of potential additions to your Community Value Statement for your organization:

- We want this community to raise awareness, brand recognition, and understanding of our product or service.
- We want this community to broaden support of our product while limiting our support costs.
- We want this community to give us better insight into what our customers want and how we can serve them.
- We want this community to build a closer relationship between our customers and the company.
- We want this community to produce a pool of potential candidates to hire.

These value statements should be complementary. *It should be clear how the company can drive value for your community members and vice versa.* Make sure this value statement is crisp, clear, and well understood by your team. It needs to get everyone's blood pumping with excitement.

PRODUCE YOUR BIG ROCKS

Communities are unusual, intangible entities that are difficult for most people to understand. While you and your team may see the opportunity baked into your value statement, this can seem wildly unintuitive for others (and generate a fear of the risks involved).

What complicates building a strategy is that communities are *cross-functional* in nature. You will need your marketing department to help with promotion and awareness. Your infrastructure team will need to spin up tools and technology the community can use. Your product team will need to interface and integrate the community into your products and services. When projects span multiple departments, it increases the risk of misunderstanding and miscommunication.

As such, gaining alignment and communication across different layers can be a struggle. You need to balance executive needs with practical guidance for the folks on the ground delivering this work. The execs don't want all the detail, but the execution staff needs a clear understanding of what delivery looks like. We need both to be successful.

The solution here is a clear set of high-level objectives, called our Big Rocks, with crisply defined owners and success criteria.

This gets everyone on the same page. Later in the book we will also craft a more detailed Quarterly Delivery Plan for the team delivering the work and for tracking progress.

HOW IT WORKS

Start by brainstorming five to seven key objectives for your community strategy that should be delivered over the next calendar year. If you don't want to commit to a year (which is my recommended time frame), focus on a six-month period. Anything shorter runs the risk of not being broad enough in terms of goals.

Right now I want to ensure you are clear on the format for the Big Rocks and what should go in them. This format is how you will document your strategy as it evolves. As with all strategic development, you are unlikely to have all the answers right now, and that is fine. Our primary goal is to be clear on this format, and ensure your team is clear on it too. This will ensure that everyone is speaking the same strategic language; a language that will ease how people feed into these Big Rocks, get their skin in the game, and align everyone with a common set of goals.

Each Big Rock should be . . . well, big. We are not looking for small improvements here, but meaty, juicy, no-screwing-around, ambitious goals. These Big Rocks should move the needle and elicit a breathy "wow" when you show them to people. Importantly, your Big Rocks should have a clear connection to generating the value in your Community Value Statement.

They should be realistic and doable. You are not going to have a 100 percent success rate, and you are unlikely to get 2 million people signed up in your first month. Think about where you are, where you want to get to, and what resources you have available to deliver it. Then add 30 percent to your goal. That'll do it.

Create a document and use the following format for each Big Rock:

- A Single Line Summary of the Objective:
  A paragraph or two that provides an overview of the objective and the primary value it will bring to the community and organization.

- Key Initiatives (over the next year):
  A bullet point list of significant pieces of work that should be performed to accomplish this objective.

- Key Performance Indicators (KPIs) (over the next year):
  A measurable set of metrics that you can use to tangibly assess if this objective was accomplished.

- *Owner:* The person who owns the delivery of this objective.

This format should be fairly self-explanatory, but I want to highlight two key components.

Your KPIs indicate the metric(s) we are using to determine success in each Big Rock.

Every piece of work in your community strategy should have target metrics attached to it, both at this larger objective level and later when we build out specific tasks in our Quarterly Delivery Plan. These metrics will keep your team on track and should be *unambiguously measurable.*

You want to be in a position in a year where we can ask "did that happen?" and be able to answer with a clear yes or no. "Maybes" are not in our dictionary. I will often break these annual KPIs down into quarterly targets to ensure the team is tracking progress actively. I have noticed consistently with clients that their teams perform better with clear KPIs (and the accountability for accomplishing them).

Speaking of which, the Owner is the person where the buck stops. It doesn't mean they do all the work, but they are ultimately responsible for corralling and cajoling people to get the work done. If the objective fails, they are the person who will have some answering to do.

Your goal here is concise readability. Let's be honest, we are all sick of reading dense, boring, strategic objectives. We don't need to know the origin of these goals. Get in, say what you are going to do, how it will be measured, and get out. *All of your Big Rocks should cover four to six pages max.*

Here are a few examples from some clients I have worked with (confidential details and names are anonymized):

Example One: User Community Growth on the Forum

Build growth of participation in our existing community forum. This is judged by both sign-ups as well as active, holistic participation based on various metrics.

Key Initiatives (over the next year):
- Full forum content plan delivered and executed.
- New product updates and key news delivered to the forum.

- Mentoring program delivered to support new members and develop their skills.
- Social media advertising campaign to point people at notable content.

Key Performance Indicators (KPIs) (over the next year):
- One thousand users signed up to the forum (assessed by both registration and confirming their account).
- Fifty percent of signed-up users (per prior KPI) post at least five topics, read at least thirty posts, and spend a total of one hour reading posts.
- Ten percent of all signed-up users (per prior KPI) visit for 50 percent of the days, have replied to at least twenty topics, and have received thirty likes and given forty likes.

Owner: Adam Hoffert

Example Two: Build an Active Support Community

Build a high-quality, reliable, community-driven support resource for other customers to get help quickly and easily from other knowledgeable customers.

Key Initiatives (over the next year):
- Design and deliver incentives and reward plan to encourage support participation.
- Notable Q&As are publicized as part of the quarterly content plan and monthly social calendar.

Key Performance Indicators (KPIs) (over the next year):
- At least 75 percent of all questions submitted receive a response (either an answer, marked as a duplicate, or marked as spam).
- Seventy percent of all questions that receive an answer have the answer approved by the submitter.
- At least three hundred customers provide at least one answer to a question.

Owner: Sarah Lewis

Example Three: Build an Engaged Developer Community

Build an engaged community of developers who are building applications on top of our platform. The success of this goal is judged by (a) how many developers we attract, (b) how many apps they produce, and (c) how well our community supports their success.

Key Initiatives (over the next year):
- New developer on-ramp designed and delivered.
- Software Development Kit (SDK) (and community integration) delivered to developers.
- Developer-focused content plan designed and delivered (including tutorials, workshops, webinars, and more).
- Best of Breed program delivered, which highlights notable apps produced.

Key Performance Indicators (KPIs) (over the next year):
- Developer on-ramp delivered.

- Version 1.0 of our SDK is delivered.
- Three hundred developers joined by the end of the year (based on registered accounts and at least one engagement with the community).
- One hundred apps submitted and approved into our app store (based on submission and availability to users).
- A 30 percent growth in traffic to our developer documentation and a 40 percent growth in traffic to our support forum.

Owner: Danielle Brescia

Rocking Out

Not sure where to start with your Big Rocks? Head to http://www.jonobacon.com and select Resources for examples. They should give you a good idea of how to build your own Big Rocks.

Notice how concise and clear these goals are. Notice that the KPIs are clear and measurable and that the owner is preferably a specific individual and not a group or department (to avoid any passing of the buck). These KPIs are not just important to ensure we set expectations and make progress, but also to ensure that our Big Rocks are delivering value.

When you have the first cut of your five to seven Big Rocks, send it out for feedback. Select a handful of key colleagues from every layer of the organization (e.g., product, marketing, engineering, support) and *ask them to be blunt and comprehensive.* Invite them to be critical; don't rely on them having the confidence to nitpick. Ask them if you are ambitious enough. Ask them if you are realistic enough.

Then . . . lock it in. *This is a sacred document.* It will be the record of what you are going to do for the next year. You invested the time in producing it, now commit to delivering it. Don't worry, we will review it periodically to ensure it is still the right plan and refine it as needed. We will cover how to do this later in the book. For now, consider this your plan of record: stick to it and make it happen.

KEEP YOUR FEET
ON THE GROUND

There are many people who effusively gush about moonshot thinking and that we should break the barriers of our thinking and expectations. The ethos of this is great: we should be ambitious, but we also need to make sure we are realistic.

Your team will have limited time. *You* will have limited time. You have limited resources available. You have limited experience in community strategy (presumably this is why you are reading this book). People get sick. People quit companies. People quit communities.

This is the human condition and we need to not be blind to it. As you design your Big Rocks, bear in mind these three key realities.

1. *Value costs money and time to create.* Oh, and it will cost more and take longer than you think. Your Big Rocks are all in service of producing this value, but when you are knee-deep in the details and execution, expect things to take longer and cost more.

You and your team are new at this, and just like learning anything new, there is a "newcomers tax." There is a cost in time and money as you and your team spin up, make mistakes, resolve those mistakes, and build skills and organizational capabilities.

2. *There will be roadblocks.* Similarly, people and things will get in the way. Key staff will quit, your various community services may not perform as well as expected, other projects will suck away resources, competitors may up their game in their own communities, and other shenanigans will manifest.

When you are planning the delivery of your strategy, factor in some buffer time to take this into account. If you have a year to do something, plan for around ten months of work.

3. *Whatever you think will happen, it will pan out differently.* Your Big Rocks put in place a firm strategy for what you want to accomplish, but as with any new strategy, the actual delivery of those Big Rocks will pan out a little differently than you anticipate. Some tasks will take longer than expected, some will be more difficult to deliver, and there may be budget/resourcing snafus.

Stick to your Big Rocks and navigate the curveballs as best you can. Try to keep the frustration at bay and instead focus on spotting lessons you can learn to avoid these curveballs in future strategies. These lessons are what build organizational capabilities and muscle: they are a good thing and they make us better.

START AS YOU MEAN TO GO ON

As you continue through this book, there are going to be a lot of new concepts, frameworks, maturity models, and other details. One of the risks of soaking up this information is that your Community Value Statement becomes a distant memory.

Avoid this at all costs.

Your Community Value Statement is the acorn from which everything else grows. Everything you do needs to have a dotted line to the *value* you want to produce. Sadly, many organizations get so wrapped up in the day-to-day tactics that they forget the bigger picture. Don't suffer the same fate.

Just like your company values, your Community Value Statement should be something you think about every week. It should be injected into the way in which you work and how you evaluate your success. You need to build a culture that repeatedly asks the question, "Is this going to help us shape the value we want?" If it doesn't, *change it.*

If you keep this value front and center, everything else falls into line.

CHAPTER 4

Humans Are Weird

I am just a human being trying to make it in a world that is rapidly losing its understanding of being human.

—John Trudell

S poiler Alert: if we want to really understand communities and how to build them, we need to understand people and how they work.

It may sound obvious, but it is astonishing how many people forget this. Businesses get sidetracked about which power tools they need (technology platforms, content, marketing, social media, etc.) and often forget about *what they are building, why they are building it, and who it is for.*

What's more, we are all guilty of lulling ourselves into our own vision of who our audience is and what they look like. We assume their character, tone, and interests, and this fiction is often based on little or no information.

One company I worked with had the most boring marketing emails I have ever seen. Dull, formal language replete with stock pictures of desks, chairs, coffee cups with "inspire someone" written on the front, and other such mundane filler.

Their customers were the opposite. Sure, they were executives in financial services, manufacturing, legal, and other areas, but they were fun, vivacious, motivated people. This company calculated that an executive audience needed plain and formal material. They were wrong. We changed it to dynamic, people-centric imagery, and saw improved engagement.

Don't make the same mistake. *We are building human systems, and we need to ensure these systems are founded on a realistic understanding of how humans actually think and behave.* You don't have to be a psychologist or have a degree in social science to accomplish this.

This work is split into three areas:

1. *Understand the irrationality of human behavior,* why we behave the way we do, and how we can harness key behavioral patterns to our advantage.
2. Decide who our audience is and *design a set of audience personas* that help us to shape our community around a realistic understanding of their needs and characteristics.
3. Finally, *understand the group dynamics in a community* so we can engage with our community members as effectively as possible.

Rather conveniently, this is what this chapter is all about. Let's do it.

THE RATIONALITY OF BEING TOTALLY IRRATIONAL

People are strange creatures. While we live in a physical world, our psychology significantly dictates how we think, how we react, and the choices we make. To put it bluntly: *our behavior is often dictated unknowingly by how we process the information we wedge into our brains.* What's more, that processing is often driven by parts of the brain forged hundreds of thousands of years ago to fuel our survival instincts and protect us from the risks surrounding us.

You seem smart. You probably consider yourself a rational, logical person, who evaluates the world around you, makes conscious decisions, and evaluates your progress regularly.

While we do make rational choices, we are also *astoundingly* irrational. Many of us drink too much alcohol, eat too many fatty foods, don't exercise enough, don't save enough for retirement, and make other choices that we know have potentially negative results. We know the risks, but we do these things anyway.

Interestingly, *many of us consistently make the same irrational decisions based on the same stimuli.*

As an example, there is the Ikea Effect.[1] If you and I were to each go and buy a MÖRBYLÅNGA table from Ikea, then go home and put it together, you would think your table is better than mine, and vice versa. Despite the fact that they are exactly the same table model, *we consistently overvalue our own creations*, and as you can imagine, this can have significant ramifications for communities and companies that have people working together and reviewing each other's work.

As one example, if we are mindful of the Ikea Effect, we can design peer review in communities to be more objective and avoid the risk of people getting frustrated because other people don't share their (overstated) feeling of value for their work.

This study of irrationality and how we make decisions is known as behavioral economics. It provides a valuable scaffolding we can use to ensure our communities are based on real, psychological human patterns and behavior. If we understand these principles, we can harness them.

A Tale of Two Brains

This may all seem wildly unintuitive to many of you. Why on earth does this happen?

Daniel Kahneman is an acclaimed psychologist known for his work on judgement and decision making. He was awarded the 2002 Nobel Memorial Prize in Economic Sciences (shared with Vernon Smith) and also wrote *Thinking, Fast and Slow*, one of the seminal books on the topic of behavioral economics.[2] In his book, he broadly divides our brain into two areas.

Our System 1 thinking is fast, automatic, and intuitive. It is our immediate, subconscious reaction to the world. This bad boy is thousands of years old, always looking for the tiger lurking in the bush, and assessing the world around us based on raw survival characteristics. This part of our brain makes us flinch when a friend sneaks up on us, makes us nervous when we walk near the edge of a cliff, and makes us scream when we fear danger.

Our System 2 thinking is the slower, analytical, dork cousin of System 1. It is always making a conscious assessment of the world and is fueled by reason and evaluation. It considers the options and makes an evaluation based on its own level of logical thinking.

Here's the key point. "The idea is that System 1 is really the one that is the more influential; it is guiding System 2, it is steering System 2 to a very large extent," Kahneman says.[3] In other words, our System 1 part of the brain is the impulsive, paranoid survivalist, and our System 2 part of the brain is the responsible, measured decision-maker.

Behavioral Economics Homework

If you are interested in learning more about behavioral economics, the following books are a great start:

- Dan Ariely, *Predictably Irrational: The Hidden Forces That Shape Our Decisions*, rev. and expanded ed. (HarperCollins, 2009).
- Dan Ariely, *The Upside of Irrationality: The Unexpected Benefits of Defying Logic at Work and at Home* (HarperCollins, 2010).
- Daniel Kahneman, *Thinking, Fast and Slow* (Farrar, Straus & Giroux, 2011).
- Richard H. Thaler and Cass Sunstein, *Nudge: Improving Decisions About Health, Wealth, and Happiness* (Penguin Books, 2009).

The SCARF Model

Behavioral economics provides an enormously valuable blueprint for one of the most challenging elements of building communities and teams: Why do people behave the way they do, and how can we tune our work to map well to those automatic behaviors?

While there are mountains of information about behavioral economics (see the highly recommended reading list above), we want to get going right away. The SCARF model was first published by Dr. David Rock, a neuroscientist, in 2008.[4] It provides five key behavioral considerations he identified from his research that are handy for us to be aware of right out the gate:

1. *Status* is important to us. Our status plays a role when we collaborate, and this affects our mental processes in many ways. We see this everywhere, from our position in our companies, to the pecking order in our social groups and family, position on leaderboards and competitions, and status with airlines.

Be very careful how you harness this. Just like in class-based societies, resentment can form between different status levels. But using status as a means to label and reward enhanced responsibilities (such as moderators, code committers, and governance members) often works well.

How to harness Status in your community strategy:

- Produce different status levels people can earn based upon clear, fair, high-quality participation.
- Reward people based on accomplishing these status levels.

- Put in place safeguards to ensure people don't increase their status without earning it and that everyone has the opportunity to gain it.

2. Certainty, and more specifically *avoiding* uncertainty, is important to our well-being. Our brains are effectively pattern-detecting machines that are trying to predict the future. When we have a lack of information, context, or understanding, it makes it more difficult to predict outcomes, and this is when uncertainty, anxiety, and stress set in.

How to harness Certainty in your community strategy:

- Focus on openness and transparency as a tool to avoid uncertainty. This should cover product updates, how the community is led and managed, how problems are solved, and other elements.
- Put in place measures to detect uncertainty so it can be addressed quickly (such as regular meetings and check-ins with active members).
- Provide a simple way in which uncertainty can be rectified (e.g., crisis response measures).
- Ensure your team is trained to be open, transparent, and provide useful information as best they can. This is key: many teams new to communities are reluctant to participate for fear of putting a foot wrong. Solve this with training and mentoring.

3. Autonomy refers to the impact of choices on our lives. Put simply, choice is important to us. No one wants to be boxed in.

Research has even found that there is positive correlation between increased choice and health.[5]

Think carefully about the choices you provide to your community members. Too limited choice is frustrating. Too much choice (typically combined with uncertainty or a lack of confidence in your decisions) can generate *decision paralysis*. This is particularly important when you present ways in which new members can participate and how they are onboarded. *The most successful communities provide many ways to participate but have simple ways of getting started.* This provides choice, but with training wheels firmly attached.

How to harness Autonomy in your community strategy:

- Provide multiple ways for people to participate, with clear on-ramps to get started.
- Provide a way for the community to give feedback and optimize how they work together.
- Allow your community to start new initiatives, teams, and projects.

4. *Relatedness* taps into the natural urge we have to form smaller tribes within a broader group of people. This is likely hardwired from our ancient ancestors living in small communities and being suspicious of strangers (who may be a threat). Not only this, but smaller groups often create a better opportunity for people to find a sense of belonging and "home."

Breaking communities into smaller teams can be a powerful way to tap into this safety instinct and build a sense of team spirit, identity, and belonging. As an example, your community may have a developer team, a support team, and an advocacy team. These naturally map to audience personas (which we will create later in this chapter), and people could join more than one team if they prefer.

This can simplify onboarding (it is easier to join a small team than a much bigger group). Be careful, though, to keep the number of teams small and the communication channels between them open to avoid silos.

How to harness Relatedness in your community strategy:

- Create a number of community teams. Start small with just a few teams mapped to personas (covered later) and grow as more people join the community.
- Mentor these teams in developing their own culture, team spirit, mascots, and more. This builds safety and belonging.
- Ensure that these teams are regularly communicating effectively with each other.

5. *Fairness* is important, not just because we want to be treated fairly ourselves but because unfair treatment elicits both a threat response, and—in some cases—a disgust response. Fairness should be a core value in communities that you build.

Seeing, providing, and experiencing fairness triggers a reward mechanism in us psychologically. It builds confidence and safety. This is a powerful principle we can harness. If we design a community that provides many opportunities for the fair exchange of value (e.g., solving problems, producing content, creating technology), it elicits an intrinsic reward response.

How to harness Fairness in your community strategy:

- Document clear expectations about conduct and participation.
- Provide training and ensure your leaders and staff follow these expectations and treat the community fairly.
- Provide clear ways in which community members can report unfair treatment and bias and have it judged objectively.

Let's take a breather for a moment. We have looked at the fundamental drivers behind why people want to join and thrive in teams and communities plus the hidden forces that influence our behavior. Now we need to get practical and start figuring out who your target audiences are and how you can design your community for them.

GETTING TO KNOW YOU (WITH AUDIENCE PERSONAS)

An audience persona is a sketch of a typical community member. They are designed to identify common characteristics and attributes with different categories of audience members.

The concept of audience personas has been around forever in marketing circles. *Personas are valuable, but some marketers tend to over-egg the pudding a little.* Frankly, I have seen ridiculous examples of audience personas so unnecessarily detailed and dense that they seem to be primarily intended for showing off. Personas need to get your team and organization aligned about who your audiences are. They are not designed to predict what kind of milk your audience puts on their cornflakes.

This defeats the whole point of producing personas. Just like our Big Rocks, audience personas are supposed to provide clarity to you, your team, and other members of your organization—in this case about what to expect in a typical audience member. Audience personas are supposed to trigger conversations about which types of audience are your priority, how you find them, and how you can delight them.

You can produce these personas by following three steps:

Step 1: Choose Target Personas

Unlike marketing personas, which often look more like a résumé of a user or customer, community personas take a slightly different approach.

Communities are fundamentally driven by active participation. This participation can be as simple as consuming information and joining discussions on a forum or as advanced as producing code that is integrated into a shared software project. The ways in which we find, motivate, reward, and engage people in a forum, and the ways in which we find, motivate, reward and engage people who write code is entirely different.

Audience personas help us to *codify an understanding of what these different types of participation look like.* How will they participate? What kinds of rewards do they enjoy? What motivates them? What are they worried about? Where do they consume information (so we know how to find them)?

To give this some color, let's take a spin through some of the most common personas in communities. This is by no means an exhaustive list and there may be additional personas you can think of that apply to you.

As you read these, think about which two to five of these personas you would like in your community.

1. *Users* are the general consumers in your community. They use your service, product, or technology. Their priority is using the product effectively and adding value in their lives. We want them to stay up to date with product news, be able to provide feedback to us, and ensure they remain loyal and happy users/customers.

2. *Fans* go the extra mile. They want to meet other fans, have discussions, and debate various topics. They provide feedback and guidance about your product and community. They often provide support too. We want our fans to be happy, motivated, and excited about our community. We want to ensure we build relationships with them (as they thrive on this validation) and always keep them excited with new features, initiatives, and ways of engaging.

3. *Support* people help other users solve problems. This may be as simple as solving individual problems for individual people, or more involved such as personal mentoring, or even providing training for multiple people. We want these people to always grow their skills (to provide broader support), deliver high-quality support, and always feel satisfied and validated by the people they help.

4. *Content Creators* produce content and material. This could be documentation and guidance about your product, blog posts

with training/guidance, tutorial videos, podcasts, material for helping onboard new community members, or anything else.

Content is powerful not just for amping up the amount of material but for generating *authentic* material. While it may lack the spit and polish your marketing team buffs into their content, community content carries *independent authenticity*. Also, it doesn't hurt that a lot of content creators are secret advocates who love to promote their work (and thus your community). We want to ensure that they are producing material that is high quality, consumed by others, that their work has a high impact, and that it is available to as many people as possible.

5. *Advocates* want your product and community to be successful. They perform marketing, outreach, and promotion to raise awareness and get people interested and involved. They are often big personalities with some familiarity with marketing and promotion. We want to ensure they have the flexibility, support, and permission to do great work (without holding them back for fear of going "off message").

6. *Event Organizers* enjoy producing and delivering events. This can include meetups, conferences, unconferences, and more. We want to ensure these people are motivated, are organizing events that are well attended, and have the resources they need to do great work.

7. *Inner Developers* write code and perform engineering that benefits a shared project in the community (such as an open-source project). We want them to enjoy solving interesting technical problems and have their contributions appreciated by the community and company.

8. *Outer Developers* build applications and services that run on a platform we run. These people usually have another primary

motive (e.g., they run a business or want to make money). We want them to produce software that adds value to our platform and accomplishes their goals (e.g., growth of their application, making money).

Of course, there are many more potential audience personas, and you can find more examples by heading to https://www .jonobacon.com and selecting Resources. Decide what contributions you are most interested in seeing and pick your two to five audience personas that reflect this. Now, let's prioritize them.

Step 2: Prioritize Your Personas

Pretty much every client I work with wants to build communities that attract *all* the audience personas that we just ran through. Why wouldn't they? They want to kick ass on all fronts.

Time for a reality check. You can do this if you want, but you will be a jack of all trades and a master of none. As with most things in life, you should *focus on quality over quantity*. Each persona requires a lot of work—each needs its own strategy, onboarding, content plan, engagement, incentives map—which we will discuss throughout the rest of this book. It is difficult to do this well for all personas (even if you throw a huge team at it, it runs the risk of being suboptimal).

You should also think about the popularity of these personas. Some personas are going to have more participants than others. For example, you are likely to have far more *consumers* of content than *creators* of content. You will have different proportions of *support* people than *translators*. Some (but not all) of these roles will also overlap, such as *support* people also being *advocates*.

It is difficult to get a sense of these proportions before you start. Take a look at similar communities and assess what proportion of members are in their target personas. Combine this with any data you may have to estimate these numbers (e.g., how much interest you may have already seen in a community) and a realistic gut check.

Taking all of this into account, you need to prioritize.

Grab your Community Mission Statement and your Community Value Statement. Based on the value you want to drive, which of the personas that you chose are most critical for the next year? *Choose two, or three max.*

No, you can't have four. Prioritization is about making tough choices. Some personas need to get cut from our focus in this coming year. Choose your two or three personas (we can revisit other personas for the following year).

For example, below could be a priority list of personas for a Champion community (in priority order):

1. *Fans*: Our top priorities are getting people passionate about our community, keeping them interested, and helping them stay engaged.
2. *Support*: We want our fans to provide high-quality guidance and advice to our users. This will be primarily focused on answering questions on a forum.
3. *Content Creators*: We want to build a range of high-quality documentation and guides and some tutorial videos. This will nicely augment the support provided on the forum.

Step 3: Create Your Personas

For each of your targeted personas, flesh them out. Create a document for each and, as usual, keep this simple, focused, and concise. *This should be one to three pages max for each persona.*

Now start filling out some key elements of each persona:

Capabilities. What capabilities do you expect this persona to have? For example, for Content Creators you should expect some prior writing, video, or audio production experience, and Developers should have programming experience. Get specific. What kind of writing experience and which programming languages and frameworks do you want for these respective personas? Be realistic: What is reasonable to expect from most people?

Experience. What experience do you expect your personas to have? This experience can be a mixture of formal (e.g., career, qualifications, etc.) or vocational (e.g., other projects, events, and experience). I recommend you primarily focus on vocational experience (e.g., which products and communities do they have experience with?) to ensure your audience is as pragmatically experienced as possible.

Motivations. What motivates this persona? What outcomes would get this person excited to participate? How do they like to see their work acknowledged? For example, Content Creators love to see their contributions published, Event Organizers love to have well-known speakers at their events and interesting (and generous) sponsors. Produce a list of these motivations.

Fears. Now flip the coin. What are the fears for each persona? What are the things they would worry about that we can try to prevent? For example, Event Organizers worry that no one will show up to their event. Developers worry about submitting broken code. These fears are important to know so we can put measures in place to avoid them.

Rewards. Now list rewards that would be interesting. For example, Content Creators who write articles love to see their work printed and framed, and Support people love to see their guidance featured on blog posts and articles. Most personas love T-shirts, mugs, and other swag. As we will discuss later, think carefully here about the logistics of shipping rewards. For example, T-shirts can be a pain as you need to have different cuts and sizes in stock.

Where They Live. Now, let's not get creepy here, I don't mean their physical address, but where do they spend their time? What websites do they visit? Which podcasts do they listen to? Which shows do they watch? Which conferences do they attend? Which social media accounts do they follow? This is especially important: it will help us find and bring our target personas to our community.

To create the most useful, accurate, and effective personas, try to depend on as much data and help from other people as you can:

- What kind of people do you see in your analytics for your website, who follows you on social media, and what do your customers like?
- Look at other communities similar to the one you want to build. Look at their different personas, how people participate, and their attributes.
- Interview members of your target persona and ask them directly what they would like to see in each persona.

- Share your personas with your colleagues, friends, and industry associates and get their feedback.
- Look at industry trends for norms. For example, find the most popular websites in your industry and identify what kind of personas populate them.

OK, let's now spin through a few simple examples to put some meat on the bone.

Example 1: Support Persona

This is Riya and she enjoys solving problems in the Acme Platform community (you guessed right; this is a fake example).

CAPABILITIES
- Deep knowledge of the product
- Experience of the product in a variety of scenarios and configurations
- Effective problem-solver. Has experience solving other people's problems
- Good communicator and able to provide guidance easily in written form

EXPERIENCE
- Familiar with online and community support
- Product experience will be variable, but fairly experienced in using it to solve practical problems (not a newbie)
- Some limited experience in online communities

MOTIVATIONS

- Product discounts
- Exclusive access to early features or unique material, content, or experiences
- Helping people
- Recognition in the community
- Broader awareness of her business

FEARS

- Providing inaccurate information
- Providing answers that may cause problems or break something
- Imposter syndrome (fear that you may not be as talented as other people think you are)

REWARDS

- Swag
- Financial (e.g., gift cards)
- Recognition and validation of her contributions

Example 2: Event Organizer Persona

This is Miguel and he enjoys coordinating events, conferences, and meetups for the Acme Platform community.

CAPABILITIES

- Coordinating and running events
- Putting together content, speakers, and other material for an event

- Working with venue, food/beverage, and other vendors
- Handling and working with sponsors and sponsorship funds

EXPERIENCE

- Has run a number of small local meetups
- Was a volunteer for a local conference

MOTIVATIONS

- Loves to bring people together
- Enjoys face-to-face engagement and in-person discussion
- Enjoys working with knowledgeable and notable speakers and sponsors
- Enjoys being in the limelight when running the event

FEARS

- That no one will show up
- That speakers are not interested in speaking at his events
- That he embarrasses himself and the community with a poorly run event
- That an event loses money (not covering costs)

REWARDS

- Acknowledgement of running great events
- Building his career experience and expertise
- Appreciation at the end of an event for putting it together
- Awards and recognition

Examples

Understanding and delivering personas is always easier to do with templates and examples. As such, I have produced a collection of personas that you can find by heading to https://www.jonobacon.com and selecting Resources.

THE TEN GOLDEN RULES FOR ENGAGING WITH MEMBERS

This chapter is called "Humans Are Weird," but communities are weird too. One of the biggest fears my clients usually have is that they are going to break some bizarre unwritten rule in how communities work.

While there are a raft of group dynamics you will pick up as you build your community experience, here are ten consistent golden rules that map to every community I have ever worked with:

1. *Your community members work for the community, not for you.* Your community is motivated by (a) their own self-interest, and (b) supporting the broader success of the community. With rare exceptions (such as internal corporate communities), this motivation is primarily directed toward serving the community, not your business.

This often trips up companies who argue, "Well, if the business succeeds, the community will benefit." Good point, but it doesn't matter. This is not how most community members think and not how the social economy works. Focus your efforts on adding pragmatic value to the community, and your business is likely to benefit indirectly.

2. *If you ask them to help, they often will.* A lot of people ask me how they get their community involved in specific projects. The answer is simple: ask them. General calls for volunteers to provide help often demonstrate limited results, but reaching out to specific individuals to ask them to do specific things often works well. Importantly though, the members are only likely to help if the work is (a) interesting to them, and (b) benefits the broader community.

3. *They thrive on personal validation and gratification.* Community members love quick, gratifying results (such as solving problems, producing content that is appreciated, running events, etc.). Similarly, they thrive on recognition of good work, particularly if it is from recognized leaders in the community (such as CEOs, community leaders, and well-respected individual contributors).

4. *They are not free labor for your company.* A common blunder many companies make is assuming this raft of community members will be interested in doing work that benefits the company such as sales, supporting customers, producing testimonials, etc. Members are unlikely to do work that benefits only your company and not the broader community. Some may even feel insulted that you asked them to provide free labor in the first place. To avoid this, ensure your personas always focus on work that mutually benefits your members and the community, not just the business.

5. *They are not sales leads.* This is important. *Don't let your sales team get their grubby hands on your community members.* If people join

the community, add value, and you reward them with unwanted sales emails, cold calls, and spam, you will irritate them (and they will likely complain about this publicly). Solve this by providing incentives for community members to come to you for sales, not the other way.

6. *They don't have the same information and context as you do.* When you work for a company that is a primary participant and investor in a community, you always have way more information than your community does. You know your staff, your customers, their motivations, the commercial dynamics and drivers, the broader corporate goals, and more.

Your community lacks this context, and as is normal with people, when information is missing, they sometimes make it up. This can result in tension (because of the uncertainty we covered earlier in the SCARF model) that can erode trust. The antidote to this is transparency, openness, and clarity. Where possible, overcommunicate features, products, policy changes, and more with the community (in an interactive way).

7. *They may share the same vision, but not the same approach.* Communities are a melting pot of priorities. Many members of your community will share your vision, but they may not share the same way of accomplishing it.

For example, when I was at Canonical, the company wanted a high-quality, successful desktop platform. This manifested in a product that we built called Unity, but some community members felt Unity was the wrong approach (due to various reasons such as the design, implementation, and other things I won't bore you with). We sought to rectify this with active engagement and discussion.

Bring clarity on the vision, but be prepared that your approach may also need some discussion. You don't need to seek permission from your community (you can channel your businesses resources however you like), but you do want to get their support and buy-in.

8. *Their commitment and organizational experience will vary.* Some community members can spend every waking moment participating in a community and some will show up for an hour here and there.

Some will want to pop in, do something, and get out. Some will be more involved in planning and structure. Provide opportunities for people to play roles with varying degrees of commitment, and don't assume everyone has the same time commitment and organizational appetite as you and your team.

9. *The quieter ones are often your secret weapons.* While there will be an abundance of vivacious personalities in your community, some members will be quieter and more reserved. It can be tempting to assume that only the louder personalities are bringing their A-game, but in many cases the quieter, less-vocal people will produce incredible value.

The key here is to engage them one-on-one. The quieter ones are often uncomfortable speaking up, so connect to them privately, get their feedback, support their success, and develop their confidence.

10. *They are your friends, and friends keep friends honest.* If your community is happy, they will celebrate your work, and if they are unhappy, they will be critical. This can sometimes tie companies new to communities up in knots.

Don't see criticism as attacks; see it as shining a light on problems that may need resolving. *Constructive criticism shows members care and is a sign of the success of your community.* Good community members will keep you focused on the problems, even if they express it rather bluntly. Require civility, not agreement to everything you do.

STRAIGHTENING OUT THE CHAOS

People don't like to be put into boxes. Sure, the world has designed different-shaped and different-sized hamster wheels for us to spin in, but many of them are ultimately unfulfilling.

Companies historically were command-and-control environments; the people at the top handed down decisions to the worker bees who followed them dutifully. This is a model that is eroding more every day. Successful modern businesses are instead seeking to strike the right balance of *leadership* and *autonomy*—it maps much more intuitively to our instinctual human drivers and psychology.

This is why communities present such an opportunity. They are a fishbowl where you can design on-ramps, workflow, incentives, and engagement that are influenced by our psychological needs *and* get rapid-fire feedback from your members on how well they work.

Communities need to be malleable in nature; they should evolve and change based on the trends and feedback you see in your members. This provides a fantastic environment to experiment and explore how to build the right balance between leadership and autonomy.

The lessons you learn don't just improve your community. They can also improve your business, member organizations, families, and more.

CHAPTER 5

Create an Incredible Adventure

I am completely in favor of dialogue and engagement.
But it must be a true, open dialogue.

—Ma Jian

I n 2014, I stepped off the BART train at Montgomery Station and walked into a friend's company situated nearby. I was popping in on my way to a client to see if I could help. I was taken into a conference room where Rebecca (her name is anonymized) sat in front of a MacBook Pro covered in stickers. She looked rather exacerbated.

"Thanks for coming in, Jono. Here's the deal. We just ran a community strategy program, hired a community manager to lead it, and invested around $110,000 in building our community. We have had a handful of members sign up and participate, but other than that, we haven't seen much for our investment. We are frustrated, our community manager is frustrated, and my boss [the CEO] is spitting fire."

I got out my computer and started looking at their community. The more I dug into it, the more I could see why this was happening. Their community was boring, disorganized, and unclear.

Their target audience was ambiguous. Their website was dull, poorly structured, and didn't help members get started. The tools required to get involved were unintuitive, complicated to set up, and required new members to jump through hoops to get anything done. Help and documentation were sparse to nonexistent, and there wasn't a place where members could ask questions. There was also barely any incentivization for helping community members to learn and grow.

Frankly, it was a mess. It was clear that their community manager had done a good job on social media and blogging, but barely any thinking had gone into shaping the overall community experience and how that impacted a community member through their eyes.

Remember that $110,000 that they invested? Just over half of it was spent on promotion and advertising to bring people into the community (to "fill the funnel," in marketing terms). This was a problem. They spent a lot of money getting people to the front door of their community, but when they got there, there were so many obstacles in their way to participate that the majority of that promotional budget was wasted. I felt bad for Rebecca; she was in a bit of a pickle.

I recommended she fix her problem by zooming out and focusing on an end-to-end community experience. There needed to be *a clear place for new community members to start, an understanding of how we keep them engaged and moving forward, and clarity on what they can get out of the experience.* This all needed to be tested with real community members, not merely members of the company, to ensure it really did make sense to the target audience.

A START, MIDDLE, AND END

On September 24, 1994, Quentin Tarantino unveiled *Pulp Fiction* to the world. While the often bloody, at times comedic, masterpiece went on to become a cult hit, at first it turned heads in the way it futzed with how the plot was presented.

Historically, writers, directors, and storytellers grew up feeding on the gruel of "every story has a start, a middle, and an end." *Pulp Fiction* changed all that. It showed the context of the ending as the movie opens, which generates curiosity about how the story would evolve, ultimately generating a more satisfying sense of conclusion when it does eventually get there.

This is the crux of great experiences. *Great experiences produce an appetite for value, set expectations, and get you there easily with gratifying results.* If we don't design a clear, logical, satisfying journey, we will lose people along the way.

Restaurants are a great example of this because there is a clear start, middle, and end of a meal, and the smooth transition through these phases has an enormous impact on our perception of the experience.

Six months ago, my wife and I went to dinner at a new restaurant in our town. From discovering the restaurant, to booking a table, to getting seated as soon as we arrived, everything ran smoothly. Our waiter was friendly and attentive, brought us water immediately, and gave us enough time to browse the menu while he took our drink orders. He provided good recommendations for their specialties, and the food came out at a reasonable cadence without being too quick or too slow. He kept our glasses full, regularly checked if we needed anything, and didn't pester us. When we left the restaurant, our opinion of the experience wasn't just based on the food (which was great!) but on the smoothness of the service, which made the entire experience *feel* high quality. We are now regulars there.

We see this with how Disney manages the guest experience and flow at their theme parks, and with how great conferences guide you from arrival to registration and then to sessions. We see it in stores, such as how Ikea guides you logically through the store from browsing furniture (and getting design ideas), to a meatball break at the café, on to the smaller items in the marketplace, and then to picking up your hulking boxes at the end before you pay.

This elegance of experience doesn't just happen in the physical world; it applies to technology too. Apple, Samsung, and Google have perfected setting up and teaching you about your new cell phone; services such as Salesforce and QuickBooks simplify getting your account set up and learning the tools; and video games such as Battlefield, Final Fantasy, and Metal Gear Solid teach the player via carefully crafted first-level tutorials.[1]

We need to take the same approach to building communities. *Don't treat your community as a loose collection of websites and content.* Think of it as a carefully glued-together chronological journey that has a beginning, middle, and end.

In this chapter we are going to put together the map for this community journey.

ROLLING OUT THE ROADMAP

The map in question is my Community Participation Framework, which I have developed over the last twenty years. It covers my approach for how to factor the right pieces in the right order into the community experience.

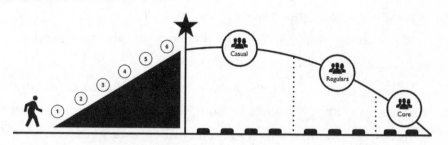

Fig. 5.1: Community Participation Framework

This framework can be applied to Consumer, Champion, and Collaborator communities across different industries, geographies, and more. It guides what I do with pretty much every company I work with.

This is the skeleton of your community. It covers the essential, foundational elements we need to include. It is designed to provide a lens we can look through to ensure we ask the right questions and include the right strategic pieces in our plans.

This framework is broken into three key sections:

1. *Onboarding*: The part to the left of the star is where we take a person who is brand new, who represents one of our target audience personas, and we help them produce something of value—both to them and the community—as quickly and easily as possible. This value is represented by the star.

2. *Engagement*: When they have produced this first piece of tangible value, they are still very new. We now help them to settle in, and support their transition between three key states: Casual, Regulars, and finally Core. This will help to grow their active participation and sense of belonging.

3. *Incentivization*: To help grow and maintain participation, we lay a series of incentives and rewards (shown by the little bumps) that help them to stay engaged, develop their experience, produce new skills, and stay motivated.

Importantly, you need to *apply the Community Participation Framework to each one of your personas individually.*

Different types of contribution involve very different ways of working and cultural norms. If you try to make a designer operate using a workflow intended for engineers, they will get confused and annoyed. The same happens when you make translators follow a marketing workflow. We want to tune our community experience to be as natural as possible for that specific persona, but also be working within a general set of tools and conventions in a shared community.

Let's now spin through these three sections and explore how they work.

NAIL THE ON-RAMP

Life is filled with journeys that involve a carefully orchestrated set of steps. These can be simple, such as filling your car (drive to the pump, pay, select fuel type, pump it, and drive off) or far more complicated such as flying airplanes, selling companies, producing records, or other endeavors.

When you build any kind of experience, you need to make the onboarding experience of the process silky smooth. The overall process should be simple, each step should be clear and lead logically to the next step, and there should be plenty of help available. This significantly increases the likelihood of a new community member getting positive results and building their confidence to keep participating.

My friend Stephen Walli, a veteran in the technology world, once shared with me that in a few companies he worked at in the '90s, a key metric for the success of a software product was the "ten-minute rule": how long it took the user to do something simple with the product from the minute the shrink-wrap was taken off the box. (The goal was, unsurprisingly, within ten minutes.) This metric was fundamentally dependent on the user understanding (a) the value the software could deliver, and (b) how to experience that value as quickly as possible.

This is exactly our goal with onboarding. For every persona you need to flip your brain into private browsing mode, put yourself in their shoes, and think about *what steps need to happen to go from zero to delivering something of value for both the individual and the community.*

Now, your on-ramps will differ from audience persona to audience persona. This isn't all that surprising: a Support persona will get involved differently than an Advocate persona, and even more differently than a Developer persona.

There is good news though. For the majority of personas, there are similar *types* of steps that occur. This is rather conveniently baked into my Community On-Ramp Model:

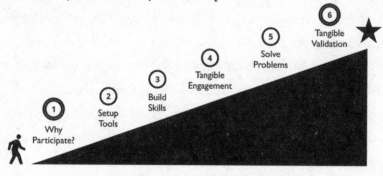

Fig. 5.2: Community On-Ramp Model

When a new community member wanders up to the start of the on-ramp, they typically progress step-by-step through six stages. Let's take a look at each.

1. *Why Participate?* Put yourself in their position. Why should they take their time away from their family, friends, and other interests to participate in your community? What's in it for them? What value (from your Community Value Statement) can you tempt them with? *You need to sell your community to them.*

At a minimum you should have a website that explains the value of participating and clear step-by-step instructions for how to get started. Support this with outreach on social media, events, and more. A great example is the Harley Owners Group, who clearly explain the benefits of joining their community, the different membership levels and perks, and more. This important step has led them to attract more than 1 million members.[2]

2. *Setup Tools.* When they decide they want to participate, people need to set up the necessary tools to get started contributing something tangible (such as an article, an answer to a question, or a piece of code). You can't build a table without knowing what a saw and a screwdriver are (despite my best efforts trying). Members need to know which tools they need and how they work, otherwise they will spend more time frustrated at the tools than doing interesting work.

In your community this may require registering an account, familiarizing themselves with a website, installing software on their computer, or other tasks. This should be as simple and pain-free as possible. In one community I saw, it took more than two hours to complete this step. This just isn't acceptable. It needs to happen as quickly as possible.

Provide them with simple instructions on how to get started, how to set up any tools, and the basics of using them. *Don't drown them in text; reassure them with simple step-by-step guidance.*

Peloton, which produces exercise equipment with live classes, is a good example. When they deliver your new bike or treadmill, they walk you through how to set it up, get you connected to their service, and show you how to get started. It is simple, clear, and effortless.

3. *Build Skills.* Now that they have the motivation and tools ready, members need to learn how to participate. This again varies depending on the persona. Provide them with the basics of how to get started in delivering value.

For example, Meetup.com is a service for organizing in-person events. They help their target persona (an event organizer) build skills with step-by-step instructions for organizing an event, and a collection of guidance in their Organizer Guide.[3]

Try to be focused and concise here: the last thing anyone wants is a raft of verbiage they won't read. *Understand what skills your members need and provide them with clear guidance so they can pick them up quickly and easily.*

4. *Tangible Engagement.* At this point in the Community On-Ramp Model they are ready to do something. Provide them with guidance on what they can specifically help with. Which questions need answering? Which events need organizing? Which features need building? How can they advocate for your community?

Provide simple ways to *connect your members with problems that need solving.* Don't desert them; help them figure out what value to add. Many new community members don't know how to get started.

As an example, many engineering communities—such as Kubernetes, Babel, Nextcloud, and React Native—point new developers at simple bug reports they can start with (often tagged with "good first issue").[4] Some support communities have lists of unanswered questions. How will this work for your community and each persona?

5. *Solve Problems.* No matter how good your onboarding is, new community members are going to hit bumps in the road while going through this process, and they will have questions and need to solve problems. Always provide a place where they can meet other members, ask questions, and get help.

This could be a discussion forum, Q&A website, or other service. Aside from just providing the resource, *reassure them that questions are welcome.* Many people new to communities are worried about looking stupid: make asking questions a normal part of the community experience.

In the beginning your team will need to field most of the answers to these questions, but as your community grows, other community members will start to help too.

6. *Tangible Validation.* Finally, when they have contributed something of value, *celebrate it.* As you can see, there is a lot involved going through the onboarding process—setting up tools, learning skills, producing value. When they successfully get through it, show your appreciation.

This can be as simple as a personal email from you thanking them, or as complex as a full rewards system and gamification (which we discuss more of in chapter 8).

Now, the eagle-eyed among you will have noticed that steps 1 and 6 that bookend the Community On-Ramp Model have a special extra circle wrapped around them. Well spotted.

This is because every on-ramp for every persona should include two specific phases: how new members are *sold on the value of participation* and *rewarding them for their efforts*. The first step is a no-brainer. You absolutely need to give people a reason to drag themselves up the on-ramp, step-by-step. Step 6 is *essential for building a sense of recognition, personal touch, and belonging.*

Again, put yourself in their position. Imagine you make your first contribution to a community and a senior member of the community or company reaches out and pats you on the back. Unless your heart is carved out of ice, this feels good. This will increase the chance you contribute again. Before you know it, participating will seem like second nature.

Before we move on to build an on-ramp, it is important to be mindful of how you validate it. On-ramps shouldn't just provide an efficient way of onboarding people. They should also allow us to verify that the member's transition between the different stages is actually working.

GET BUSY WITH YOUR AUDIENCE ON-RAMPS

Now, pull out your audience personas and design each one its own on-ramp. Feel free to base this on my Community On-Ramp Model, but you know your community goals better than I do; don't be constrained by my model.

As you create each on-ramp, start thinking about what kind of tools, documentation, and resources you might need. Also, reread your Community Value Statement and try to engineer as much of that value as possible while new members traverse up your on-ramps.

Here are a couple of examples:

Support On-Ramp **(help for a streaming TV device):**

- *Why Participate?*: A community website showcasing benefits of participation, stories of positive community experiences, social media, and broader outreach.
- *Setup Tools*: Registering an account on the forum, knowing where to find the list of current questions, and knowing where to find other tools and documentation.
- *Build Skills*: Learning how to use the forum, how to respond to topics, how to create new topics, where to find questions that need answering, and how to reference external materials.
- *Tangible Engagement*: Finding and answering support questions in the community forum and ensuring answers are accepted.
- *Solve Problems*: Mentoring from other community members on how to effectively provide support.
- *Tangible Validation*: Email recognition of their first answer being accepted and a thank-you note from the community leader.

Outer Developer On-Ramp **(building applications for a mobile platform):**

- *Why Participate?*: What is the value of building an app for this platform and what are the tools, resources, and support that are available to make it as easy as possible?

- *Setup Tools*: How to set up the Software Development Kit (SDK) and create a new project.
- *Build Skills*: Documentation for how to learn the SDK and the Application Programming Interface (API), and how to submit applications to the platform for review.
- *Tangible Engagement*: Building and delivering an application for review.
- *Solve Problems*: Where to find documentation and how to ask questions on a community forum.
- *Tangible Validation*: When an app is accepted for publication, members receive a simple care package in the mail (T-shirt, mug, note) and a thank-you email from the community leader.

As you design your on-ramps, I want you to avoid some common landmines buried in the process. Let's spin through each.

Don't assume too much. Don't assume your audience has the information you have and don't assume they have much community experience. You *should assume impatience.* Your community members should expect to get results quickly, so ensure your on-ramps are fast and efficient, with little-to-no bureaucracy.

Start simple and iterate. Sometimes the best tool is a hammer, not an electrical power tool. As you design your on-ramps, always ask the question "can we make this easier for them?" In the majority of cases the answer should be yes. As French writer Antoine de Saint-Exupéry said, "Perfection is finally attained not when there is no longer anything to add, but when there is no longer anything to take away."[5]

Every step should connect clearly to the next step. The very best journeys and the very best on-ramps make every step and how they connect crystal clear. For example, when someone has learned the skills in step 3, connect them directly to where they can do real work in step 4, such as a task list.

Where possible, every step should be measurable. We want to track down where the problems lie in our onboarding. If lots of people get to step 3 and then drop off, we know there is a problem with the transition between steps 3 and 4. Try to find ways to measure when a user has completed each step. This can help resolve any problems that bubble up to the surface.

Test all your on-ramps objectively. When you have your on-ramp designed, find people who match the target audience persona and have them try it. Ask them for their feedback. Invite blunt criticism. Watch them go through it, then find the bumps in the road and fix them. It is astonishing what you will learn from watching people try your on-ramps.

Amp Up Your Audience Personas

Want to see examples of on-ramps for different audience personas? Head over to https://www.jono bacon.com and select Resources.

ENGAGEMENT

The majority of community members whom I have met benefit from clear guidance and guardrails to be successful. They may be hard workers, smart, motivated, and enthusiastic to succeed, but they generally need someone pointing them in the right direction.

For example, in the corporate world this generally happens when staff have an assigned manager. This person is expected to be your go-to for ensuring you are able to succeed in your role. While not all managers are good at this, there is clear accountability in place.

It works quite differently in communities. Typically, when you join a community there is no manager and no specific person responsible for your success. *You*, the member, are responsible for your success. As such, your community should be as simple and intuitive as possible from the get-go so members can benefit from it immediately. This should span from your on-ramps all the way to how you engage with them. In a perfect world, every community member would have a mentor to guide them. Since that won't scale, there are three approaches I recommend to get people up and running:

1. *Self-direction* provides the right set of choices to your community members, where they can always find new things to do and accomplish, all of their own volition. Video games have new quests and objectives. Fitbit has new fitness challenges.[6] Jeep has new Jamboree events to join.[7] StackOverflow showcases interesting questions that need answering.[8] Think about how your members can always find something interesting to do.

2. *Peer support* provides ways in which members can support and guide one another. The American Physical Society provides a formal mentoring community.[9] Many engineering communities have code peer-reviewed before it is accepted. We used to run Ubuntu Open Week, which provided peer training and Q&A

sessions.[10] Consider structured ways in which members can provide input on another member's work.

3. *Incentivization* is where you provide specific incentives and rewards that keep people moving forward. Again, in video games this often happens when players are rewarded with trophies, in-game equipment, or new features as they complete various challenges. We will cover incentives extensively in chapter 8.

You should integrate all three of these approaches into your community. Bring your team together and start brainstorming ideas within each of these three areas. Now, let's go back to the Community Participation Framework:

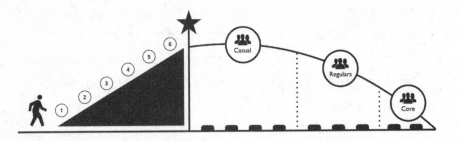

The portion to the right of the star is where we focus on building *engagement* in the community.

In my framework, we break the overall community experience into three segments: Casual, Regulars, and Core. This break down is not something you generally publicly label in your community (e.g., *Jack is Regular, Polly is Core*). It is a way in which you and your team internally evaluate where different members are in the journey.

Each of these segments represents three different psychological states that people are in as members and how we can adapt our engagement to them based on their state.

The eagle eyed among you may have spotted that these different segments are proportional in size. As a general rule, *for every one hundred community members, seventy will be Casual, thirty will be Regulars, and one will be Core.* You can rustle up your own math to see how these proportions may map to the size of your target community. Remember, your broader audience is also out there, including those who may lurk, watch, and observe until the inspiration strikes them to contribute (and thus wander up the on-ramp).

Our ultimate goal is to wire together the right mixture of self-direction, peer review, and incentivization to keep them progressing from Casual to Regular, and then from Regular to Core. *Not everyone will want to ultimately get to Core, but you should build an environment that supports this transition if they choose to make it.* Let's take a look at each of these different segments.

Casual

When a community member has progressed up their on-ramp and generated something of value for themselves and for the community, they become a Casual member.

Casual members are fragile creatures. They may have had a single success going up the on-ramp, but they generally don't know most people in the community, they are unfamiliar with most of the tools and processes, and they often won't get the in-jokes. They have a long road to travel, but that first success has given them the energy to keep going.

If you remember the SCARF model back in chapter 4, we humans are not exactly fans of uncertainty. Many casual members feel socially awkward, don't feel comfortable speaking up, and often suffer from imposter syndrome (where you feel you are inferior and you will get "found out" by your peers).

The major goal with casual contributors is to help them acclimatize and settle in. Help them solve their problems. Build their confidence. Provide them with mentoring and guidance. Help them discover simple-to-follow ways of participating and getting involved. Help them to get to know other members, build relationships, and develop friendships.

Casual members have variable levels of participation (hence being *casual*). While they may participate somewhat randomly, they will often be watching what others are doing very regularly. It is common for people to lurk before they participate.

To get them to be a Regular, help them build a habit. *It takes around sixty-six days to form a habit, and your goal is to get them participating throughout that sixty-six-day period.*[11] When we build habits, things that were once complicated and that we needed significant mental energy to accomplish become easier and more natural. We see this in our daily lives with eating well, exercising regularly, mindfulness, and other areas.

Regulars

When a new member has participated for a *significant and sustained period of time,* they can be considered a regular. Now, it is up to you to determine what "significant and sustained" is within the context of your community.

Regulars are the bread and butter of your community. If you treat them well, they can provide years of dedicated participation and service.

The key goal here is to ensure they are *informed, equipped, and can participate without too much red tape.* One of the problems a lot of companies face is that, as they grow, they introduce more checks, balances, and approvals into the general community workflow. Unless this is carefully monitored, this can drive your members nuts.

Your Regulars will also be developing a lot of experience in your community, developing respect from other members, and getting to know you and your team more. For many, their appetite to be involved will be growing. They will want to be more involved and will appreciate when you provide the opportunity to include them.

Find ways to incorporate your Regulars more and more into the broader structure and strategy of the community. Invite some of them to meetings and get their feedback on how to make improvements. Invite them to events. Ask them for guidance. Ask them to help with specific projects. Run your strategic plans past them. Ask them to help mentor other members, and more. This all continues to seal that critical sense of *belonging* which will continue to build long-term participation and retention.

Core

Core members are your major leaguers. They provide a foundation to your community. You know them by name, and you have enormous respect for the sheer amount of time and devotion they provide to the community. You and others think of them as rock stars and worry from time to time what would happen if they left.

How do you know who these people are? Simple. You pick them by hand. These are the people who you immediately think of as being your most committed and dependable community members. They come in all shapes and colors. In one community I worked with, one of their Core members was seventeen years old. His age didn't make a difference; he did amazing work.

Every community has a handful of these Core members. Not all of them agree with you, and some will be critical and hold you accountable. This is a good thing. Don't surround yourselves with sycophants; that's not how you grow and learn. These people work hard, keep you honest, and add enormous value.

The major goal with Core contributors is to make them feel part of the leadership of the community. When we trust people, we lean on them more and trust their judgement more. When possible, include your Core contributors in strategic meetings. They have enormous insight, and they will see your community from a different and deeply valuable angle. You are too close to the flame, and you need their mentoring and guidance.

Give them the white glove treatment. Treat them with the respect they deserve. Build a personal relationship with them. Send them gifts on their birthday. Offer to help where you can with their career and wider goals. Take them out to dinner, buy the expensive liquor, and always treat them with sheer dignity and respect.

I cannot underscore enough the importance of treating your Core members well, but more importantly, really leaning on their expertise and guidance. *Listen to them. Learn from them.*

Many community managers make the mistake of treating all their community members in a subservient role. Don't make this mistake with your Core members. Be vulnerable and ask for their help and guidance; you will benefit from it.

INCENTIVIZATION +
REWARDS = GROWTH

Let's take a moment to zone in on the little bumps you see at the bottom of the Community Participation Framework. These are the incentives that you will plumb in throughout the Casual to Regular to Core journey.

These *incentives and rewards are designed to keep people interested and motivated to keep participating*. They will be a mixture of automated detection as well as specific campaigns, events, and invitations.

The idea here is simple: if you place a regular series of incentives and rewards along the journey from Casual to Regular to Core, and those incentives reward positive contributions and behavior, it naturally keeps people moving forward.

This is similar to how Fitbit awards you badges for reaching daily goals or lifetime achievements, how The Coffee Bean Rewards app gives you free drinks for earning points, and how you earn air miles with United by using one of their credit cards. It all keeps people interested and engaged.

Hold that thought for now as we get into this in detail in chapter 8.

CREATE AND MANAGE A
QUARTERLY STRATEGY

As we continue through the book and add pieces to your strategy, you need a way to capture this work. Sure, the Big

Rocks cover your broader objectives, but how do you manage the nitty-gritty details wrapped up in the day-to-day delivery of this work?

Welcome to the Quarterly Delivery Plan. It looks like this:

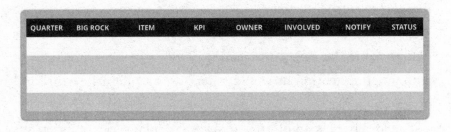

Fig. 5.3: Quarterly Delivery Plan

This can live in a spreadsheet or your chosen project management system.

The idea is simple. You list each of your *BIG ROCKS* and break them into a set of individual *ITEMs* that deliver the goals of each Big Rock. For each item, specify a set of *KPI*s that state clear, measurable deliverables to be completed for that item.

Each of these items is then assessed as to when it can be delivered, and a *QUARTER* is selected. This gives a clear idea which items for which Big Rocks will be delivered and when.

Accountability is critical. Far too many companies put together a plan and then bicker over who will do what and when. Get this clarity up front through this document, but also ensure that your team knows that they are expected to deliver. Plans mean nothing if people ignore them or are chronically late without good reason.

For each item, have a single *OWNER* who takes responsibility for delivering that item. This doesn't mean this person does all the work, but the *buck stops with them*. If the item is not delivered on time and delivering the metrics in the KPI, the owner should have some explaining to do.

In addition to the owner, the people or teams expected to be *INVOLVED* in the delivery of the item are added, as well as any people to *NOTIFY* when the item is complete, delayed, or postponed. This is helpful for ensuring that various team leads and stakeholders are kept up to date without being involved in the nitty-gritty details.

Finally, you can use the Quarterly Delivery Plan to track the current *STATUS* of these items on a weekly basis. I suggest you have the following set of status options that you select to reflect how far along the item is:

- *Not Started*: No work has started on the item yet.
- *In Progress*: The item is currently being worked on.
- *Under Review*: The item is complete, but it is being reviewed to ensure it meets expectations.
- *Complete*: The item is complete.
- *Delayed*: The item is delayed for some reason.
- *Blocked*: Progress on the item has stopped due to something else being in its way (which needs unblocking).
- *Postponed*: The item has been postponed and may or may not be rescheduled for a different quarter.

Here are a few examples for items on the Quarterly Delivery Plan:

Quarter	Q3
Big Rock	Build a Predictable Support Community
Item	Deploy Forum
KPI	Identify and select forum platform
	Deploy online (available via desktop and mobile)
	Allow login via Google, Facebook, and Twitter
	Configure key categories (General Discussion, Q&A)
Owner	Rebecca Bergmann
Involved	Stuart Langridge, Tom Draper, Jeremy Garcia
Notify	Erica Brescia
Status	In Progress

Quarter	Q4
Big Rock	Build a Predictable Support Community
Item	Produce Core Documentation
KPI	Documentation available on the community website for:
	Getting started guide
	Support best practices
	Transitioning material to FAQs guide
	Mentoring program overview
Owner	Lee Reilly
Involved	Margot Maley, Tim Carter
Notify	Simon Bacon
Status	Completed

This Quarterly Delivery Plan is not the only way to manage communities, but I strongly recommend it. It ensures every item ultimately maps to your broader value, is resourced, is scheduled appropriately, and avoids ambiguity for what should be delivered. It provides a single place for everyone to track progress and keep people accountable. With many of my clients, this plan is designed for the execution staff, but the senior execs like having the ability to view the current status of work if they want to.

As we wander through the rest of the book and cover different strategies, they should ultimately end up on the plan. One surefire way to reduce risk in communities is to ensure that your work is carefully managed and tracked.

As you build out your plan, there are eight important principles you should incorporate:

1. *Always ensure items have a clear dotted line to a Big Rock.* You need to avoid the temptation to throw things on the strategy unless it drives direct value to one of your Big Rocks (remember our Big Rocks have their own dotted line to our Community Value Statement). Sometimes items won't have a clear, direct connection to a Big Rock, so scrutinize these more carefully. They could be distractions.

2. *Ensure your team is accountable.* One of the biggest failures with strategic planning is a lack of accountability. I see it daily with some companies. If you want your strategy to succeed, the owners of items need to be on the hook and accountable if there are problems or failures. Similarly, those involved need to plan for their involvement and not wimp out with "Sorry, I just don't have time due to excuses A, B, and C." If you are leading this work, *it is* critical *that you bake this accountability (and appropriate resourcing) into the process.*

3. *Be realistic about delivery.* Look at the KPIs required and the available people in your Involved column. Can those people realistically deliver that set of KPIs (while being mindful of their other day-to-day responsibilities) by the end of the target Quarter? If not, scale the work back.

When I see many of the same names listed in the Involved column across multiple tasks, it is a red flag that those people may be overstretched. Can other people replace or help them?

4. *Ensure it is a "sacred document."* Plans only work when everyone sticks to them. If they are ignored or changed on a whim, it renders them about as useful as a chocolate coffee pot. This document should be sacred. It should be everybody's priority, always open in their web browser, and looked at daily. Be careful with making changes once the plan is in place. We will discuss how to do this later.

5. *Review progress weekly, resolve problems, and update statuses.* One of the flaws with many project plans is that people make the plan and then immediately forget about it. To avoid this, have a regular weekly meeting where you review the plan and current statuses. Look for items that are delayed or blocked and try to resolve those. Ask the team for any problems that are slowing them down or getting in the way. Again, we will discuss this later in the book.

6. *Review and update at the end of each quarter.* Let's be realistic: businesses, communities, and people change and adjust. Needs and requirements change, and you need to be reactive to this. At the end of each quarter review the overall plan and make any adjustments.

This commonly involves refining KPIs, retargeting work to different quarters, switching team members in and out, and introducing new pieces of work. Try to avoid making these changes mid-quarter. Otherwise it compromises how sacred the document is (see number 4 above).

7. *Create a backlog.* There are always more things to do than time and resources available (unless you can conjure up some dragons

to do the work for you). This doesn't mean you can't track the work for future delivery though.

I strongly encourage that you add items at the end of your Quarterly Delivery Plan that need to be done in the future—just don't assign them to a Quarter yet. This way you can document the work needed but schedule it when the resources and time open up.

8. *Use failure and delays to spot opportunities.* Life isn't a flowchart, and things get in the way. It is not a matter of *if* some things will be late, it is a matter of *when.*

When you experience these problems, look for *why* they happen. As an example, when I ran my team at Canonical, we had a six-month chunk of work, and around 30 percent of the items by one of my team members were late. Instead of raking him over the coals, it was clear to me that he was working hard, but he took too much on. For the next cycle I helped him improve his estimation of work, and he nailed his delivery. *Failures are opportunities for improvement if you are willing to look for the signals.*

A FIRM FOUNDATION, BUT KEEP THE TROWEL IN YOUR HAND

At this point you may be feeling a little overwhelmed by how much work needs to be done. The Community Participation Framework looks like there are lots of different pieces of work buried inside it, and you are not wrong. There *is* lots to do, but the good news is that it doesn't all have to happen at once.

Think of the Community Participation Framework as the schematic for a building we want to build. Just like building a house, we start at the foundations and gradually build up from there. You don't have to have all the answers—in fact, it is almost impossible that you *do* have all the answers. As we continue our journey through the book, we will keep building on these foundations until we have a strong base.

Reid Hoffman, cofounder of LinkedIn, once said, "If you're not embarrassed by the first version of your product, you've launched too late."[12] He is spot on. Don't wait until you have all the answers before you start building your community. Let your intuition guide you, but ship something. Deliver work that you can evaluate, evolve, and expand. This is how we get better and how we build great communities.

CHAPTER 6

What Does Success Look Like?

Before anything else, preparation is the key to success.
—Alexander Graham Bell

I have a confession to make: I am a recovering idealist.

When I was a long-haired (believe it or not), leather-jacket-clad eighteen-year-old, I drove to nearby Northampton to nervously join my first community meeting. It was focused on a technology that I had become interested in and took place at the home of a nice chap who set up the group.

That evening was eye-opening for me (in a good way). I saw the power of people having a shared passion, but one integrated into a global community focused on having a real impact. It unlocked in my mind the real potential of people.

Enthusiasm in the human condition can also be a risk though. It is tempting to fall into the creepy abyss many self-help authors descend into in which they believe *anything* is possible despite the realities and constraints in the world. *While our ambition should be bold and brave, it should also be grounded in realism.* We need to understand what success can realistically look like. This is what this chapter is all about.

RISKY BUSINESS

Let's cut through the BS. Communities are risky. Any initiative that involves people working together is risky. When you glue people, platforms, and processes together, all manner of things can go wrong.

Your community may be boring and uninteresting. You may struggle to get people interested and involved. The community may produce uninteresting results or barely any results at all. People may get into arguments and spats. Your infrastructure and technology may be absent, broken, or unreliable. You may have political issues to wrangle with between different teams, people, and ideas.

Risk is a spectrum with two extremes. One side views the world as a place full of risk, and all they do is seek to avoid or react to it. The other sees a world full of potential and opportunity and seek to harness and grow it.

We can't be either of these people; we have to be both. We need to understand the risks, be motivated by the opportunities, and have a clear sense of what we can accomplish within this cocktail. We accomplish this in four ways:

1. Assess and understand the value we want to produce.
2. Put a clear plan in place to accomplish that value.

3. Know what we need to measure and measure it effectively.

4. Set reasonable expectations on what success looks like based on our measurements, and adjust our strategy where needed.

The Einsteins among you will have noticed we have already focused on numbers 1 and 2, and now we need to zone our radars in on numbers 3 and 4. Let's start with one of the most misunderstood and error-prone elements of not just communities but businesses and management in general: *measuring effectively.*

IF IT ISN'T UNAMBIGUOUSLY MEASURABLE, IT DOESN'T EXIST

I want you to do one of the following: Grab a piece of paper, book into a tattoo parlor, or hire an airplane and memorialize this by word, ink, or giant flapping banner: *"If it isn't unambiguously measurable, it doesn't exist."*

Every team I work with understands the importance of measuring and assessing work, but many are unable to measure their work *unambiguously* with the goal of using that data to drive changes and success. I see a lot of goals like:

- *"Improve* the website."
- "Build customer *growth* this year."
- *"Speed up* our customer onboarding process."
- "Make the sales process *more efficient."*

These are all ambiguous, and *ambiguity is both subjective and risky*. Subjectivity isn't usually a problem when everything is going well, but when the results are looking grim, people will zone in on the "improve," "growth," "speed up," and "more efficient" and claim their understanding was radically different. Excuses, excuses, excuses.

We are not in the business of excuses. You didn't buy this book to do just OK. You bought this book to kick ass. The only way we kick ass is with clarity of strategy, execution, and lessons learned.

From a *strategic* perspective, we have already focused extensively on clarity. We have shaped our Community Mission Statement, the value we want to drive, our Big Rocks, and our Quarterly Delivery Plan. As we execute, we need to measure your work and performance with purpose. To do this well, I suggest you follow my Four Rules for Measuring Effectively.

Rule 1: Test Critical Dimensions

Projects and initiatives are the major areas of investment for businesses. Critical dimensions are the key areas in which you measure your effectiveness in delivering projects and initiatives.

These critical dimensions are present in every product, service, and community. In a car they can include speed, safety, comfort, and storage capacity. In a computer they can include performance, stability, storage, and connectivity. In a community there are seven primary critical dimensions that I see in most cases (not in any priority order):

1. *Growth.* How many people are joining your community? How is the growth changing over different time periods?

2. *Retention.* Of those people who join the community, how many are sticking around and participating?

3. *Community ↔ Community Engagement.* How are people collaborating together? Are they engaging and working together?

4. *Company ↔ Community Engagement.* How effectively are your staff engaging with the community?

5. *Delivery.* Is the community delivering results within that audience persona? For example, are Support personas answering questions, are Developers producing code, and are Content Creators producing useful content? Is the community delivering value in your campaigns and initiatives?

6. *Attendance.* How well attended are your in-person events, online webinars, campaigns, and other initiatives?

7. *Efficiency.* How efficient are your various processes such as your onboarding, collaboration processes, conflict resolution, and other elements?

As an example, if one of your Big Rocks is to build a thriving online support community, you should track how many people join (*growth*), the quality of their support (*community ↔ community engagement*), how long they stick around the community (*retention*), and how effective your support persona on-ramp is (*efficiency*). This will keep you on the right track.

Use these dimensions as the core of how you track performance, but don't be afraid of adding more dimensions *if* you don't have another way to track your work objectively. Be careful though: if you ask humans to accomplish certain numbers, often their singular focus becomes those numbers, even at the expense of the spirit of the work. This makes picking which critical dimensions to address even more important: ensure they provide a holistic picture that can't be artificially gamed.

Rule 2: Measure Both Action and Validation

Many moons ago I joined an early online forum. I signed up and was given a "n00b" badge (nerd slang for someone who is a "newbie"). The next badge up ("curious"), required me to post two hundred messages to the forum. The one after that ("regular") required me to post another five hundred posts. This was common in forums and sadly is to this day in some corners of the Internet.

As you can imagine, this system was easily abused. People would often respond in the minimal socially accepted way to get their post count up. It was common to see responses to discussions with little more than "I agree," "LOL," or " :-)." These responses added nothing to the discussion or the community; they decreased signal and increased noise.

The problem here was that the forum measured only the *action* of posting something. What it didn't measure was the *validation* of that thing: whether the action is any good or not. While not always the case, many actions have a companion validation that can, even in a loose sense, help determine whether the action is any good or not. For example:

- A user can sign up for a service (*action*) and then sign-in and do something (*validation*).

- An answer to a question can be posted (*action*) and then selected as the answer (*validation*).
- A piece of code submitted (*action*) can be peer reviewed and merged in (*validation*).
- An event that is delivered (*action*) can get a positive review from an attendee (*validation*).

As a general rule, tracking the *action* is a great way to measure *engagement* and *delivery*. Tracking the *validation* is a great way to measure the *quality* of that engagement. Focus on tracking both where you can.

Rule 3: A Matter of "Yes" or "No"

Cast your mind back to chapter 5, and this baby should look familiar to you:

QUARTER	BIG ROCK	ITEM	KPI	OWNER	INVOLVED	NOTIFY	STATUS

This is where we track the specific pieces of work that deliver the goals in our Big Rocks. The most important information to track here is your KPIs. There are countless books and seminars on how to produce effective KPIs, but I am going to boil this down into something very simple. When you ask the question "Did we accomplish this," it should be answerable with a clear "yes" or "no," and not a "maybe."

This is all about listing specific, measurable KPIs. "One thousand community members signed up within a year" can get a yes/no answer. So can "Support on-ramp is completed on average within two hours."

On the other hand, "Build solid community growth" and "Deliver efficient support on-ramp" are ripe for darts with "maybe" written on the side to be lobbed at them. *Be specific. Be measurable.* Demand that every KPI has a "yes" or "no" answer. "Maybe" is a cop-out, and you are better than that. Keep thinking of new KPIs until you can weed out any and all "maybes."

I have noticed consistently with clients that when there are clearly measurable KPIs, their teams perform better. Most people need concrete goals. Make sure you get your KPIs right.

Rule 4: Limit What You Measure

Fasten your seatbelts, I am going into rant mode.

One of the flaws in the human condition is to focus on the *appearance* of doing something well. People buy fast cars and expensive clothes to appear successful. Bureaucrats add layers of process to appear responsible. Similarly, people completely overdo metrics to appear that they have their finger on the pulse of their community strategy. This is a waste of time, energy, and money.

I can't tell you how many companies I have worked with who take the approach of *one dashboard to rule them all.* They are of the view that we *may* need to measure something in the future, so we need to measure every conceivable thing.

There isn't anything inherently wrong with tracking lots of data, *if*—and this is a big *if*—you stay focused on converting that data into actionable outcomes. If you have five hundred graphs in your dashboard, you have five hundred things to get distracted by, and at least five hundred conversations to have. Those graphs will not all map to your critical dimensions, and most won't map to your Big Rocks. Throw them out.

Our solution here once again is simplicity and a simple formula:

Big Rocks + Key Critical Dimensions = KPIs

If you have five Big Rocks and you are tracking two to three critical dimensions in each, those are the things you need to measure. Obviously don't be too anal about this; you may need to track other things, but stay focused on which items are ultimately delivering value to your Big Rocks.

With the majority of new clients, I suggest they only track a few critical dimensions. We are better focusing on five metrics than fifty. This keeps you focused, simplifies your discussions, and ensures your batting average is going up as you execute this work.

DON'T JUST GET ON THE SAME PAGE—STAY ON IT

Life pro tip: *all great work needs a strong, dependable foundation.* This applies to constructing buildings, designing high-quality products, or building communities.

This is why we have built a strong foundation using the tools we have already discussed such as our Community Mission Statement, Community Engagement Models, Community Value

Statement, Big Rocks, Community Participation Framework, and Quarterly Delivery Plan.

When you combine these with clear maturity models and a cadence-based workflow, they help clarify what success is and how you can measure it. Confused? Don't be. All will (hopefully) be clear soon.

There are three key areas in which you need to track success:

1. *Productive Participation.* At the center of a strong community are productive, happy, community members. We have already defined our Community Value Proposition and Audience Personas. How do we ensure our target personas are accomplishing that value?

2. *Getting S#!t Done (Delivery and Execution).* We have already broken our Community Value Proposition down into our Big Rocks and then started pulling together our Quarterly Delivery Plan. How do we ensure our strategy is working well and getting delivered?

3. *Organizational "Oomph."* Finally, the success of your community will be directly related to how well you bake community strategy and engagement skills into your organization. It is essential we track this organizational skills development.

Let's dig into each of these key areas.

Defining Success 1: Productive Participation

One organization I worked with wanted to build a community of authors who would contribute to their shared service. Like many companies, they had already taken a shot at building a community and their results were fairly average.

"What do you want to see these authors accomplish when they join the community?" I asked while sipping down my morning coffee. My answer was met with a stony silence. They knew they wanted them to produce content, but they didn't know *what* to expect in the stages between "no content" and "lots of content."

This is why we developed our Audience Personas back in chapter 4. It gives us a clear idea of the *type* of participation we want to see. But how do we know if we are serving those audience personas well?

To help with this you can use my Community Persona Maturity Model shown in figure 6.1:

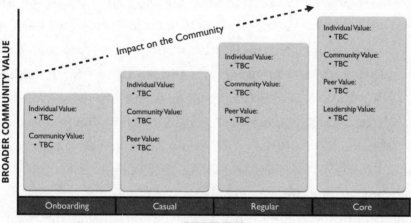

Fig. 6.1: Community Persona Maturity Model

For those of you new to maturity models, they provide a simple way of defining what success should look like at a given time. They are a common tool used by overpaid plastic-haired business consultants, and sadly many of them are so generic that they are useless. This Community Persona Maturity Model is what a maturity model should look like (if I do say so myself).

Here's the key point to remember: *maturity models show you the framework of what to measure, but you need to fill in the details yourself.* If you are expecting me to be able to precisely tell you what you should expect with a given persona for your specific community, you will be sorely disappointed. The only way to accomplish that is to hire me. Communities are just not that generic and cookie-cutter. Instead, an effective maturity model provides an overlay to look at your community through the right dimensions. You will need to fill in the details yourself based on your context, expectations, and aspirations.

Here's how it works. Along the bottom axis you can see the phases from our Community Participation Framework back in chapter 5. It includes the Casual, Regular, and Core segments, but it also includes Onboarding, as this is a critical component of assessing success. For each segment we define what success should look like. This is measured using a few different dimensions.

Individual Value. What is the *measurable* value that this persona should deliver for themselves? As an example, for a Support persona in our onboarding segment, this could be "Posted a question to the community and received an answer that solved the problem."

Community Value. What is the *measurable* value that this person has brought to the community? Again, for a Support persona in the onboarding segment this could be "Answered a question in the community that solved the problem for a member."

Peer Value. What is the *measurable* value that the person has provided to help their fellow community members? For any persona in the Regular phase this could include "Delivering one-on-one mentoring to at least five different community members." This could also include training, providing community leadership, or producing documentation to help others succeed.

Leadership Value. What is the *measurable* value the person has given in providing leadership in the community? For any persona in the Core phase, this could include: "Representing a board seat in a community governance council for a one-year term."

Those of you who continue to be eagle-eyed may have noticed an emphasis on *measurable* in the above examples. In case our earlier discussion of the Four Rules for Measuring Effectively didn't hit home, go and read it again. Now, to be fair, you can also cut yourself some slack here: these don't need to be as finitely measurable as KPIs, but it should be clear whether they have been achieved or not.

You may notice on the Community Persona Maturity Model that some of the above dimensions appear on some of the columns but not others. This is because the way in which we assess these different community phases (Onboarding, Casual, Regulars, Core) will differ depending on the phase.

For Onboarding we want to stick to our original stated goal in chapter 5 of helping them to deliver a single piece of value for themselves and the community. As such, you should be measuring a single accomplishment within that particular persona.

For example, for an Engineering persona this could be:

Individual Value: Fixed a bug or added a feature that the member needed.

Community Value: Made a code contribution to improve the product that was accepted.

For Casual we want to measure meaningful-yet-casual partici-pation. This is often small and transitory. It could be answering a question, fixing an issue, or providing a small piece of content.

For example, for a Support persona this could be:

Individual Value: Answered a single question that has been accepted by the asker with an appreciative reply.

Community Value: Solved a problem faced by a community member.

Peer Value: Provided limited mentoring to a single community member.

For Regulars, this is often similar to Casual contributions, but they provide more consistent and sustainable contribution, and they often work on larger and more comprehensive pieces of work (because they have more proven faith in the community).

For example, for an Engineering persona this could be:

Individual Value: Resolving bugs and adding features on a monthly basis that serve their needs.

Community Value: Consistent monthly contributions of code to the shared project.

Peer Value: Providing code review and technical input on other people's contributions (thus improving overall quality).

Finally, for Core, we build on Regulars, but with an added focus on consistent participation, increased responsibility, mentoring, and leadership capabilities.

For example, for an Author persona this could be:

Individual Value: Consistent monthly articles published for an extended period of time (eight or more months).

Community Value: Consistent monthly contribution of content and education that is highly rated by members.

Peer Value: Consistent monthly feedback on other people's written work in the form of editing and mentoring.

Leadership Value: Has measurably optimized the overall writing and submission process, supporting resources, and how content is published and consumed. Has also helped the company in other areas of community strategy, problem-solving, and support.

More Persona Success Examples

Need more examples? No problem. Head to https://www.jonobacon.com and select Resources.

Defining Success 2: Getting S#!t Done

The very best companies I work with can have the greatest plan in the world, but some members of their teams will struggle to stay on top of it. They will also struggle to know when is the right time and circumstances to make sensible adjustments to the plan. This is just human nature when working on new initiatives with already busy lives.

The solution to this is *cadence-based cycles*. This is something we used at Canonical for Ubuntu, and it worked well. Various other companies and projects use a similar approach. It looks like figure 6.2:

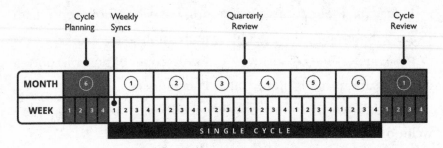

Fig. 6.2: Cadence-Based Community Cycle

What you can see here is a timeline broken into months and weeks. Each cycle is two quarters, six months. You can see each month numbered 1–6, and on either side I included the last month of the previous cycle and first month of the following cycle (those are shown in gray).

We created our Big Rocks back in chapter 3 that outline the value we want to produce for the next year. This year is comprised of two six-month cycles, each of which delivers half the work in our Big Rocks. Now, based on figure 6.3, let's cover what happens in each six-month cycle.

Before our cycle begins, in the month before, we perform our Cycle Planning. This is where we plan what work we want to deliver for the next two quarters (which combine to form the full six-month cycle).

This is when we map out our Quarterly Delivery Plan from chapter 5. Based on your Big Rocks, fill out what you want to accomplish in these next two quarters, complete with KPIs and the other items.

Each week we need to stay on track in delivering the work mapped out in this quarterly plan. To do this, coordinate a weekly call with everyone who is listed in the Owner column in the Quarterly Delivery Plan. This is where you ensure everyone is up to date, discuss any problems, ensure everyone is able to keep moving forward, resolve any items that are blocked, and keep making forward progress.

At the end of the first quarter, you perform a quarterly review. Remember, you are half-way through your cycle, but you want to ensure that the plans you have in place for the second half of the cycle (the next quarter) still make sense.

Review the items in your Quarterly Delivery Plan, and take a good, hard look. Are your Big Rocks delivering the value you hoped so far? If not, tweak the individual items based on what you have learned. Refine any KPIs, owners, or assignments. The goal here is to make relatively minor refinements: we are still focused on delivering our Big Rocks. We just want to optimize them and ensure that our plan still makes sense and we are making the most out of our available teams and resources.

At the end of the first cycle, do a thorough review of everything so far. This review should be a broader meeting with key stakeholders, other departments, or even certain board members and investors. *The goal is to ensure we are still making the right strategic bets and not blindly sticking to a plan.*

Ask critical questions including, but not limited to:

- Are you making progress on your Big Rocks? *If not, why?*
- Are your individual initiatives delivering value? *If not, why?*
- Are you accomplishing your KPIs and other target metrics associated with the work? *If not, why?*
- Are your community members happy with this work? *If not, why?*
- How is your team working together? *If not well, why?*
- Do you need to adjust resourcing or personnel?

- Is this work delivering the value in your Community Value Statement and moving the needle on your Community Mission?

This review should be honest, blunt, and frank about both the successes and the failures. *You should come out of it with a set of improvements you want to put in place in the next cycle*, both in terms of work and also how the team works together.

Importantly though, *celebrate your successes.* If you only ever focus on improvements, it can suck the fun out of the work. When you get something right, pour some bubbly, celebrate with your team, and make them feel good.

Now build out the plan for the next cycle, which should be the second half of the time period for your annual Big Rocks. Repeat the same cycle: produce your next two quarters in your Quarterly Delivery Plan, again ensuring that your KPIs all lead toward your Big Rocks.

Refer to the improvements you identified from your cycle review and integrate them into the plan for this forthcoming cycle. This provides a way to directly make improvements every six months.

I have found that time and time again, this cadence-based approach doesn't just keep everything on track but also builds familiarity with these different milestones. Once you have run the cycle a few times, you and your teams will anticipate when to plan work, have quarterly reviews, stay on track with weekly meetings, and review and optimize each cycle based on how well it went.

Defining Success 3: Organizational "Oomph"

Some organizations new to community strategy just want to learn the hacks to do something that gets results. Real success in building communities is dependent on integrating the skills needed to plan for, grow, engage, and optimize your community experience. To do this you need to not just execute but build new organizational capabilities. This is the focus of our final maturity model.

There are three stages in which an organization develops these new capabilities.

First you *incubate* new skills. You build an environment with the right mix of resources, education, strategy, and execution that (a) brings in new skills, (b) trains people in them, and (c) supports them as they apply those skills.

Look, you are going to screw up. You will make mistakes, which is fine. *Incubation is all about experimentation and discovering what works and what doesn't.* You have to allow this experimentation to thrive in controlled conditions (which is our overall community strategy).

We then focus on *intention.* You take the lessons learned in the incubation phase and become intentional about them. You produce organizational Standards of Practice, train people in them, and ask people to refine and evolve them. This generates your internal playbook for how to do this work well based on your growing experience.

Finally, you *integrate.* You take these best practices and solidify them across the organization. Many companies that fail at community strategy do so because they restrict it to a silo. As an example, an entertainment company I worked with had one person who managed their community program. That person effectively ended up becoming an ambassador to the community. Other staff assumed that this Community Director was doing the work and that they could safely forget about the community and get back to their normal day-to-day.

Don't do this.

Trust me, it is not a winning strategy. The companies that succeed are the ones who *integrate community strategy across the business, aligned with product, engineering, marketing, and sales.* Your organization, and how it interfaces with the community, should be a clean, well-oiled machine, and this is the last phase in organizational maturity.

We combine these three phases with a targeted set of Areas of Expertise, and we start to see what our maturity model looks like. I call this my Organizational Capabilities Maturity Model, and you can see it in figure 6.3.

Organizational Capabilities →			
	1 INCUBATED	**2** INTENDED	**3** INTEGRATED
STRATEGY	Coordinated strategic planning/execution.	Regular structured planning cycles.	Strategic evolution and execution.
MANAGEMENT	Clear community management in place.	Team growth and mentoring.	Fully performing org. department.
GROWTH	Initial growth strategy formulated.	Experimentation with growth hypotheses.	Growth patterns identified and evolved.
ENGAGEMENT	Engagement by community team/staff.	Engagement broadened to other key teams.	Engagement an org. performance req.
LEADERSHIP	Leadership by specific team/staff.	Company & community stakeholders involved.	Broader governance bodies in place.
TOOLING	Community tools are available for use.	Tools integrated into broader org. resources.	Tools are a key part of product/eng. roadmaps.
METRICS	Metrics tracked for target personas.	Refinements and action taken regularly.	Community metrics part of overall KPIs.

Fig. 6.3: Organizational Capabilities Maturity Model

As you can see, there are seven rows, each of which represent an Area of Expertise. Each area spans across our three phases, and it provides an opportunity to specify what we should expect to see for that Area of Expertise in each phase.

For example, with Strategy, you should expect your Incubation period to include organized, structured planning (as we have discussed throughout this book). When you become Intentional though, you should see repeated planning cycles (as we discussed earlier) happening over and over again. Finally, at the Integration phase, you should be evolving your strategic cycles, refining and optimizing them for not just *what* work we want to do but *how* we do that work together.

While the criteria I provide in figure 6.4 are what I generally recommend for most communities, be sure to tune this to your specific needs. Book a meeting and ask your team the question: How should we refine Jono's criteria in his Organizational Community Maturity Model for our specific organizational goals in the next year?

These seven Areas of Expertise are the most critical and common areas I see in organizations I work with across a wide range of communities. Let's look at each of them:

1. *Strategy* refers to the organized way in which you convert your Community Value Proposition into a real, living, breathing community. It incorporates much of what we have discussed so far—our Community Mission Statement, Big Rocks, Quarterly Delivery Plans, various maturity models, and how we run and tune these cycles.

2. *Management* refers to how you facilitate and run your community. This incorporates community management, how it is

integrated into your organization, team growth, resourcing, and other elements that relate to building and maintaining an effective community management function in your organization.

3. *Growth* refers to how you build growth and participation in your community. It focuses on discovering and identifying patterns, developing hypotheses for growth, and integrating critical patterns across the community. Growth is very dependent on individual communities and circumstances: this is about adapting our strategy based on what you see in your organization.

4. *Engagement* refers to how you engage with the community in a personal, predictable, and positive manner (which we will cover in depth in the next chapter). In the earlier phases, specific individuals primarily engage with the community, but you want to build this out across your organization. You also want this to be fun, engaging, and dynamic, not a mind-numbing snooze-fest.

5. *Leadership* refers to how you lead and run the community. In the earlier stages, you will do much of this directly, but you should grow and integrate community leaders into your strategy. Ultimately, you may want to explore independent governance to provide additional objective leadership that operates in the best interests of the community.

6. *Tooling* refers to all the tools, infrastructure, and other nuts and bolts that make your community machine purr. In the earlier phases this will probably be its own little community island, but as it becomes more mature, it should be tightly integrated with product and engineering teams. This will ensure the community platforms become a part of your organization's overall product and experience.

7. *Metrics* refers to building maturity in how your organization measures your community, its health, as well as how to evolve your strategy based on what you see, measure, and understand. Again, you should get this to a point where community performance is tracked organization-wide and reports up at a senior level as a critical component of how the organization functions.

As with everything in this book, you should consider all of these models, frameworks, and approaches like a recipe in a cookbook. Use it to make your dish, but then adapt to taste. Experiment, try new things, add additional Areas of Expertise, and tune it to fit you.

The Organizational Capabilities Maturity Model is only as effective as it is deeply wired into your organization. If you only put it up on a screen, point enthusiastically with eyebrows raised, and never look at it again, you are wasting everyone's time. You know who enjoys their time being wasted? No one.

I typically follow five rules for applying this maturity model with most companies:

1. *Review at the end of each cycle.* At the end of each six-month cycle, review the Organizational Capabilities Maturity Model and assess if there are any shorter-term changes you should make to continue forward progress. This should include the most critical teams involved in the work.

2. *Do a full strategy review once a year.* At the end of each year, perform an in-depth review of the Organizational Capabilities Maturity Model with your leadership team and key departmental staff. This should be a fundamental meeting designed to identify key gaps that need filling. We will cover more of these key gaps in chapter 10.

3. *Gather feedback from all layers of the organization.* When you review your progress, be sure to gather feedback from a multitude of different departments. For example, don't just invite the engineering team to discuss the *Tooling* area of expertise. Bring key departments in: you will get better input. *We want buy-in on this work, but that buy-in needs to be real.* Many meetings end with nodding so people can get out of there. Ensure that their agreement is authentic.

4. *Emphasize a desire for critical feedback.* The biggest risk of using maturity models is that you are uninformed about what is actually happening and therefore unable to optimize how things work. If you are running the community strategy, or are a C-level executive, you *are probably already uninformed* as some people simply won't share some things that are happening on the ground. *Make criticism unambiguously welcome and reward people for it.*

5. *Integrate changes in your* Quarterly Delivery Plan. As you identify areas of improvements to be made, break them down into specific pieces of work with owners and track them in your Quarterly Delivery Plan.

THE PATH IS UNPREDICTABLE, BUT NOT UNMANAGEABLE

When I was eighteen I left school with a distinctly average set of grades. When I studied my GCSEs (the exams we covered in my core education in England), I averaged out with Cs. I went on to A Levels (the education between school and university), and I got two Ds, an E, and an N. I think an N meant I spelled my name wrong on my damn exam paper.

My journey from there was nonlinear. I discovered the open-source community, started writing articles for magazines, became a casual journalist, then got a job as a consultant based on an article I wrote. From there I built a reputation, joined a hot up-and-coming company, and one thing led to another throughout my career. Not everything in life is a four-step plan.

This chapter provides guardrails to the seemingly windy road of successfully coalescing groups of people together, but be realistic in this journey. *Sometimes these models won't perfectly map neatly to your specific community and you will have to think on your feet.*

That is a good thing. Again, the best chefs don't just follow recipes. They use the recipe to get a head start, but then they experiment and discover their own style and technique. Do the same with these approaches to success. They are a firm foundation, which you can refine and tune to build something truly incredible.

CHAPTER 7

Glue People Together to Create Incredible Things

Great things are done by a series of small things brought together.
—Vincent van Gogh

A few months ago I was pacing the Oregon Convention Center in Portland. It was Monday, the day after I had run one of my conferences, the Community Leadership Summit. As I leaned against the side of a coffee shop sipping my overpriced convention-center brown muck, a familiar face wandered over and uttered, "Alright, mate!"

Adam (his name has been anonymized) was similar in age to me, and I met him when he was involved in a previous community I worked with. He gushed about how he learned and grew his skills, that other members of the community gave him great feedback, challenged his assumptions, and helped him to improve. He reminisced over the early days of meeting new friends and how many of those friends went to his wedding, have met his kids, and have spent long weekends at his holiday home with him. He summarized it with, "I wouldn't be here today in this convention center if it wasn't for the community." It was that community's *predictable, positive, personal culture* that had this impact on Adam.

Communities can be remarkably empowering, not just for public communities but also internal communities. I worked with two different banks, both struggling with teams that were not collaborating together and staying in their silos. I helped them each build a shared community space where they collaborated on projects, provided peer review, organized skills-development events, and shared insights. Their productivity didn't just increase—their teams were also *happier* working together.

I did something similar with a large Chinese firm. We didn't just provide a shared working environment; we also gamified it so employees would be both rewarded and recognized for their great work. We even had posters of notable employees dotting their campuses. Again, a collaborative culture was something their employees wanted, and the results demonstrated it.

Here's the rub though. *Cultures are hard to understand and build.* They are formed from *a set of norms that are repeated and become adopted by the broader group.* As such, we want to build a set of cultural norms in your community but ensure that they are adopted, embraced, and evolved by your community, not merely shoved down their throats.

In this chapter we are going to delve into how to build a community culture and how to build growth and engagement while doing so.

BUILDING A CULTURE

To build an effective culture, you need to take a structured, strategic approach. We will do this by focusing on four areas:

1. *Understand the Ten Culture Cores.* Just as in music, writing, art, theatre, or other art forms, the tonality of how you do something is as important as the mechanics of doing it. As discussed earlier, your community should be *predictable, positive*, and *personal.* With this in mind, we need to ensure our tonality, voice, and approach are balanced. I have developed Ten Culture Cores you can use as a guide.

2. *Build a Growth Strategy.* You can't build a community if there is no one around. We need to build a growth strategy that helps people understand why our community is interesting and why they should join us. This will get people through the door and onto our Community Participation Framework.

3. *Build an Engagement Strategy.* As our community forms, we need to engage with them, keep them motivated, and maintain their enthusiasm and interest. To do this we need to provide a regular stream of engagement that is *personal* and *productive.*

4. *Observe, Hypothesize, Experiment.* As you deliver your growth and engagement strategies, you should observe what is happening based on the visible results, develop new ideas to improve and refine, and experiment and test those ideas. This is how you not only tune your community but also build community strategy skills in yourself and your organization.

As we bundle our way through these four steps, we are going to use the different pieces you have already baked into your community strategy. This will include your Community Mission Statement,

Community Value Proposition, our Audience Personas, and your Big Rocks. As we identify things we need to do, you can track it all in our Quarterly Delivery Plan.

UNDERSTAND THE TEN CULTURE CORES

Miles Davis, a legendary jazz musician, once said, "It is not the notes you play; it's the notes you don't play."[1] With communities and cultures, it is often the things you don't say—the unwritten norms—that generate the biggest impact.

This is one of the hardest elements for me to train in organizations. *There is a lot of subtlety wrapped up in the tonality and approach of how we engage.* Subtlety is difficult to teach and requires practice.

These are ten rules (in no particular order) that I recommend you and your team follow. Read them, digest them, and practice them. Discuss them with your colleagues. They are your values: their fabric will help your community to be a kind, compassionate, and engaging place.

1. *Be open.* Always default to open where you can. Be open in your communication, decision making, how you evaluate choices, and how you reach conclusions that affect the community. *Talk and write openly and freely, provide extra context, and overcommunicate.* It will reduce anxiety, build relationships, and build trust. It will set the norms of how those who participate engage.

This is easier said than done, particularly for employees. Many companies new to communities will have reluctant staff who are worried about putting their foot in it and accidentally sharing confidential information. Provide training, mentoring, and assurances that your team won't be punished as they learn this openness. Give them time to adjust, but require this kind of openness.

Openness breeds *authenticity*, which has been a constant throughout this book. Your community and its members don't just need authenticity, they respect it. This all needs to happen out in the open, but it can be difficult in challenging times.

Mike Shinoda is the cofounder of the music group Linkin Park, who have sold more than 70 million records and won two Grammy Awards. Mike has been a consistent architect of communities over the years and has been very open in how he approaches his work. He is also just a bloody nice guy.

In July 2017, this openness faced a critical moment. His friend and singer of Linkin Park, Chester Bennington, sadly passed away and was mourned by millions. Mike, who was grieving his close friend, faced a decision about how to approach the Linkin Park community and what his balance of openness would look like.

He shared with me his thought process:

> In the big picture, you have to do things that feel right to you, that tell the truth, and that might be important or useful to people. To that end, when Chester passed away, it put everything in my career and personal life into turmoil. I didn't know how much of my personal reactions and feelings I should share publicly. I found myself taking some time away from the public for a few months, focusing on making art—songs and paintings—in order to sort through my thoughts and emotions. Those songs and paintings ended up being a perfect way to communicate

my perspective on everything, and I put them out as an album called 'Post Traumatic.' It felt like letting the whole world read my diary, which is a very exposed feeling.[2]

Mike handled it perfectly. He took the time he needed but never lost his connection to his community. He continues to inspire not just me but millions of others. Rest in peace, Chester.

2. Be pragmatic. Too many communities are *all talk and no action.* One local community I knew spent six months debating what platform their new website should run on. They obsessed over it instead of just making a decision and moving on.

Avoid unimportant, rambling, nonproductive discussions. Your community should be in the business of *getting s#!t done* (while having a great time). Trade in specific, actionable work with specific outcomes. Work toward measurable value, not obscure or irrelevant ideas.

3. Be personal. One of the major challenges that communities face as they grow is illustrated in figure 7.1:

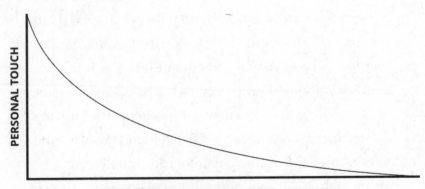

Fig. 7.1: Community Personal Scaling Curve

Often as a community grows, there is a desire to automate more. Common tasks, workflow, and engagement are replaced with automated emails, forms, and other computer jiggery-pokery. This reduces the personal touch as the community grows.

People don't join communities to talk to computers; they join communities to talk to *people*. Always focus on a personal level of service and interaction. Get to know people, their lives, their families, and their interests. *Focus on quality not quantity.* It will build better long-term health in your community.

I worked with a large company who struggled with this personal touch with their employees. To help rectify this, they encouraged employees to set up "interest communities." Before long, groups focused on running, gaming, weight loss, leadership, music, and more sprung up. It required very little company resources, but it got employees mixing together around common interests and helped erode silos. Some of the strongest relationships were started in those interest groups.

4. *Be positive.* Part of the reason tonality is so important is that it rubs off on people. *Highly positive environments generate positive engagement,* and negative environments result in a bunch of Debbie Downers, who precisely no one wants to be around. Be positive, encourage your leaders to be positive, and it will rub off. This should be reflective in your writing, content, emails, and beyond. Having a bad day? Pull it together. Put on a bright smile and keep the positivity flowing. This will ensure a stable positive foundation.

5. *Be collaborative.* Communities are formed on a foundation of sharing and collaboration. When people avoid these cultural norms, they can be culturally criticized (and potentially ousted).

Try to avoid decisions being made in a silo. *Involve people, gather their feedback, get a gut check, and validate your ideas.* Coordinate community members. Invite feedback on planning documents. Again, people won't judge you just on the decision but also how you made it. Involving and including people always reflects well.

If you do have to make decisions confidentially, try to set expectations in your community. Make it clear there is a dividing line, but provide the best context you can on how decisions were made. Try to keep the information flowing as much as you can (such as around release dates, new features, and policy changes).

6. *Be a leader.* Don't be afraid of being a leader. Some new community managers are scared to lead for fear of alienating people. If you focus on our other Culture Cores, such as being open and collaborative, you don't have to worry about this. Most people need good leaders. Be one.

Leadership will also involve making some tough choices. *Don't be afraid of unpopular decisions.* You are not Dr. Evil. Do your best to ensure they are the right decisions, get a gut check from people you trust in the community, and be open about how you reached those tough choices. You will earn respect, even in the face of unpopular choices.

7. *Be a role model.* In the same way positivity or negativity rubs off, so does leadership. It is not just your decisions that leave marks but also how you reach them. Demonstrate objective, empathetic, authentic decision making and leadership. *Be the person you want to be and you will be the leader other people want you to be.*

8. *Be empathetic.* Communities are a melting pot of people from different backgrounds, experiences, and levels of expertise. We need to be mindful of these differences and demonstrate empathy to their experiences. We have done this previously when we put our brains in private browsing mode: we looked at things from their perspective.

If people disagree with you, struggle, have problems, or don't understand you, be empathetic. Look at it from their perspective, and demonstrate this to them. *Be intentional: don't just be empathetic in the privacy of your own mind. Say it, demonstrate it visibly.* This all builds trust. Empathy is a powerful driver for building inclusion, which is a powerful driver for innovation.

I first met Ali Velshi, a thunderingly sharp and affable news anchor for MSNBC, at an event we ran while I was at XPRIZE. He spends his world knee-deep in our political discourse and sees the importance of empathy and inclusion in communities both broad and narrow. "Communities allow for inclusive conversations that don't deny our inherent individuality, but allow platforms for discourse that permit us to explore our commonalities."[3]

He underlines this potential, though, with an apt caveat, "Belonging is crucial to us as individuals, but civility is crucial to us as a society." Ensure you don't just show empathy yourself, but develop a culture of empathy across your members too.

9. *Be down-to-earth.* People always identify with and like others who they feel are "on the same level" as them. This means identifying with other people, leaving your ego at the door, and always demonstrating humility. *Let other people sing your praises; it is for them to decide, not you.*

Focus on building relationships, being interested in other people and their lives, and how you can support their success. Don't just focus on the people you can get something out of. Don't just focus on "important" people. Humility to those at every level of your community builds mounds of trust and results in shared stories of those positive experiences.

10. *Be imperfect.* You and I are both imperfect. We screw up. We make mistakes. First, acknowledge this, get used to it, and embrace it. Second, talk about your imperfections, seek counsel from others in how to improve, and share your learnings from failure.

The worst thing you can do is to present yourself as having all the answers. You don't, and people will respect you more if you are open to the fact that we are all learning. *Treat the community as an experience you are shaping together with them, complete with all the successes and failures therein. It will build fantastic commitment.*

Review these Culture Cores again. Review them with your team. Discuss them, understand them, and debate them. Make them the foundation of how you operate; it will help you shape a more human and humane community.

BUILD A GROWTH STRATEGY

Back in chapter 2 we talked about the referral halo. If you walk past a restaurant that is empty, you are likely to keep on walking. If you see a bustling restaurant with a free table where people seem to be having a blast, you are more likely to go in. Validation by other people provides this referral halo, which encourages us to make similar decisions, such as getting killer pizza.

Momentum made this happen. Psychologically, you observed numerous other people seemingly having a positive experience, and it validated the premise of it for yourself. This is why we read reviews on online shopping websites, why pop musicians continue to grow in popularity as they become more successful, and why Internet memes develop. If you are able to build momentum, you are able to more easily build growth.

Let's explore how to first launch your community and then build growth.

Plan a Kick-Ass Launch

The first step in building growth is to launch your community. Sadly, far too many organizations silently launch their communities into the world. There is no fanfare, no excitement, and no launch. *This is a grave mistake.*

For the majority of launches, I recommend five key components. As you build these out, be sure to add them to your Quarterly Delivery Plan.

1. *Infrastructure and Content Finalized.* Ensure all your community infrastructure, services, and sites are up and running. Also, make sure any promotional content (such as blog posts, press releases, videos, etc.) is ready to go. If it is not ready, be sure that you have a clear content plan with authors assigned to produce that content at prescribed dates.

2. *Early Adopter Program.* Always run an Early Adopter program first. This is where you first invite ten to twenty people who you know and trust to the community to have private access and provide feedback before you fully launch. Carefully consider who these people are: they will likely become leaders in your community.

I did this at XPRIZE when we launched the Global Learning XPRIZE community. We invited around sixty Early Adopters, and they didn't just help us to refine the community but also played a critical role when we ran a $500,000 crowdfunding campaign and ultimately raised $942,000.[4] They produced content, provided feedback, performed advocacy, and more.

Your Early Adopters should be people who are passionate about your success and motivated to be in your community. They are typically passionate existing customers, users, associates, and friends.

Inviting these people serves a few important purposes. First, they can test out your community, find any problems, and report back to you what needs fixing before you launch. Second, it provides a great opportunity to include them in the design and optimization of your community. *Get their feedback, ask them questions, ask them to help with promotion.* Third, when you take the wraps off the community, you will already have some momentum formed (by these Early Adopters) so your new community doesn't look like a ghost town.

When I do this I usually invite them a few months before launch and emphasize that we want them to play a critical role in helping us to shape the community. When you invite them, ask them to join a kickoff event or webinar a month before your public launch.

At this event/webinar you can get them motivated about the community, share your goals, and get their feedback. Be clear in what you expect from them, how you want them to participate, and what kind of guidance you need from them. Also, at the same event/webinar give them access to the community and provide a demo for how they can get started.

3. *Teasers Launched.* A month before launch start posting public teasers to keep people guessing.

Get creative. Garmin launched a mysterious countdown clock.[5] Virgin Red released a mysterious blurry video of Richard Branson on Twitter (complete with a hashtag for people to discuss it).[6] There are lots of ways to get people excited.

4. *Announce a Launch Event.* A few weeks before launch announce the launch event. This event should be no longer than an hour and

provide an overview of the community, some key content/demos, interviews, and an open Q&A for viewers. Announce the event and what will be covered.

5. *Launch Day.* Run the launch event and coordinate any press to be launched on the same day.

Here is a broad timeline I recommend you work from:

Timeline	Item
T-Minus: Six Months	Full launch strategy complete, with KPIs, owners, and delivery dates.
T-Minus: Three Months	Early Adopters identified (ten to thirty recommended). Target press identified.
T-Minus: Two Months	Contact Early Adopters and invite them to private kickoff event/webinar. All community infrastructure is ready for launch.
T-Minus: One Month	Early Adopter event/webinar. Invite Early Adopters to the community. Gather feedback and input. Make improvements and changes. Start public teasers.
T-Minus: Two Weeks	Announce launch event.
Launch Day	Launch event/webinar featuring overview, interviews, and how to get involved. Press interviews and momentum. Kick off your Growth Plan (see below).
Launch + Two Weeks	Reward Early Adopters who have provided outstanding service (send them swag, gifts, etc.). Highlight notable early members of the community.

Table 7.1: Community Launch Timeline Template

Create a Growth Plan

A launch is designed to generate an intensive burst of awareness and energy. With momentum as your core focus, you need to follow this launch with clear, consistent amplification that results in growth. If you take your eye off the ball after the launch, everything will fall flat.

There is no single growth strategy. Building growth requires a multimedia approach. *Growth brings people in, but engagement makes them stick around.* Let's explore effective growth strategies. These individual activities should be tracked in your Quarterly Delivery Plan.

Content and Editorial: Content is a fantastic way of building growth. New communities typically face an *awareness gap* (people learning what your product/community is), and a *skills gap* (how to get involved). Content can close these gaps and bring people to your community.

You have to be organized, though. I once worked with an educational platform client who said, "Let's set up our blog, social, and other resources, and just write content as we go."

Don't do this.

Life got in the way, and they went weeks without material. *You need a constant drip-feed of material to bring people into your community.* Plan this work in an Editorial Calendar that maps out the next twelve weeks (three months). This calendar should provide a place to track when the content should be delivered, when it is published, and who is assigned to produce it, as shown in figure 7.2:

DELIVERY DATE	PUB. DATE	TYPE	ITEM	AUTHOR	STATUS	NOTES

Fig. 7.2: Editorial Calendar

As with our Quarterly Delivery Plan, track the delivery of this work in your calendar via the Status column.

Sit down and brainstorm enough content ideas that you can deliver the following minimums:

- *Original blog content:* One per week (material you produce about your product/community).
- *Original social media content:* Three per week (social media you produce about your product/community).
- *Blog content promoting other material/content:* One per month (material that promotes interviews, articles, podcasts, and other things you participate in).
- *Social media promoting other material/content:* Two per week (social media that promotes interviews, articles, podcasts, and other things you participate in).
- *Themed campaign:* One per quarter (competitions, campaigns, content series, and other initiatives).
- *Online event:* One per quarter (webinars, demos, Q&A sessions, and more).

Ideally you should have all content for your prelaunch, launch, and postlaunch brainstormed, approved, and complete with assigned authors at least three weeks before your prelaunch. This material doesn't have to be complete, but it should be in a plan.

As you brainstorm this material, *cover the key topics that your target audience personas will find valuable.* Put each idea into your editorial calendar, find someone to produce the content, and set target delivery and publication dates. Ensure those people have a calendar invite to know when their material should be delivered: everyone needs to stay on track or the overall plan is at risk. An editorial calendar is a powerful tool. *Get creative with how you generate content*:

- Produce fun and interesting demos (e.g., a client of mine showed how their product could be used to automate a morning ritual, such as brewing coffee, powering on a microwave, and playing music).
- Invite yourself on other people's podcasts and video shows, write guest articles, and speak at other people's events (this provides a way to reach out to their audiences).
- Do interesting and thought-provoking talks at conferences and in online webinars.
- Run competitions and contests that get people submitting content (e.g., writing, apps, videos). For example, HackerOne had an online hacking competition with prizes to attract new security researchers.[7]
- People love building interesting things. Post tutorials to show how people can do interesting things in your community or

with your product/service. The *Make:* community does this, such as their article for how to make LED earrings.[8]

- Make short documentaries, how-tos, video interviews with your community, or other fun and engaging snippets.
- Brainstorm and track it all in your editorial calendar. Remember, *content drives momentum*!

Need Creative Inspiration?

No problem! For more ideas and examples of interesting content, head to https://www.jonobacon.com and select Resources.

In-Person Events: Meetups, conferences, hackathons, and other in-person events are a fabulous way to raise awareness and build growth.

As we cover in-depth in chapter 9, events can also be a money pit. One mistake I see many communities making is hiring a community manager and flying them around the world hitting up every conference possible. This is expensive, time-consuming, and makes your community manager less available and more jet-lagged.

Be judicious, target your events carefully, and squeeze the maximum amount of value out of them. We will cover this more in chapter 9.

Advertising: While rarely used for communities, advertising can be a useful tool for raising awareness. Focus it on promoting specific pieces of content and events and ensure there is a clear connection from that content to the beginning of your on-ramp.

Review where your audience personas consume information (you put this together back in chapter 4). Do a limited test-spend on some of those resources (e.g., spend $100 to promote a specific article on a specific social network). Evaluate the results and identify which material and approach works better. Now do another test-spend and try to get the performance up. When you feel you are getting decent performance, put in place a broader investment.

Incentives and Rewards: Clear incentives and associated rewards are a fantastic way to bring people in. Hold your horses—we will cover this in detail in chapter 8.

BUILD AN ENGAGEMENT STRATEGY

Back in chapter 5 I introduced you to my Community Participation Framework:

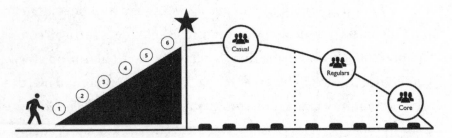

As we discussed, the community journey is broken into three key phases: Casual, Regulars, and Core. I once worked with a client who built a community around their business management platform. We had a guy called Siddharth proceed up the on-ramp and answer his first few questions in the community forum. He became a Casual member and helped provide guidance from time to time. He was great. Gradually, he started to become a Regular, appearing on the forum most days and also writing help documentation, organizing local events, and other activities. Before long he became a Core member, helping to optimize our on-ramps, incentivize members, provide mentoring, and more.

Just like Siddharth, our goal is to *keep community members moving forward,* progressing from Casual members to Regulars, and then on to being Core members of our community. There are two primary ways to keep this forward progress.

First, produce a series of incentives that keep the journey interesting and rewarding. We will discuss this extensively in the next chapter.

Second, *engage with them, interact with them, get to know them, build relationships, and support their broader success.* Engagement is not about any specific task. It is about providing the right cocktail of encouragement, support, and guidance. Engagement differentiates the communities that merely work and the communities that *thrive.*

The Journey from Casual, to Regular, to Core

Our Casual, Regular, and Core phases provide a way for us to understand the nuances of the community member's psychology and needs at the different points in their community journey.

These phases apply to pretty much all communities. For example, both a hardcore technical community and a knitting community will have Regular members. They will both have similar traits for a Regular member (e.g., significant and sustained participation), but with obviously different subject matter.

Let's take a look at these phases and how you can engage with them:

Casual: Our number one goal with Casual members is to *make them feel at home and help them be successful.* There are four key ways to do this:

1. *Be responsive and help solve their problems.* First and most critical, be *ultraresponsive. Whenever a casual member posts anything, keep the conversation going.* If they ask a question, provide an answer. If they ask for an opinion, share one. If the conversation dries up, keep it moving.

In the early stages of a community, building momentum is absolutely critical. To be blunt, this requires awkward small talk as you generate discussion and engagement. I coached a new start-up through this a while back. I asked them to ask their new community members for feedback and suggestions, and what they would like to accomplish in the community. I encouraged them to brainstorm, get excited about an idea, and pursue it. Within six months the start-up saw their community jumpstarting a new marketing initiative and website.

In the beginning most of this engagement will come from you and your team. As momentum builds, members will talk to each other and you can take your foot off the gas a little (but you still need to stay focused on members).

2. *Validate and celebrate their efforts.* When they contribute to the community in some way, validate and celebrate great work. Be effusive in how their work has helped the community, how they are making a difference, and how you appreciate them. This validation will significantly increase the chances of them continuing to participate. If their work is subpar, give them positive but constructive feedback to help them improve.

3. *Break the ice and build a relationship.* Where appropriate, break the ice and get to know them. This isn't all business; if you detect a shared interest, discuss it. Ask them what their broader goals are in the community and help them get started. *Always emphasize that you are there to help.* It is this personal touch that builds trust and then momentum.

4. *Help them find opportunities to make an impact.* Many Casual members want to make a difference but they don't know how to get started. Don't hesitate in suggesting things that you think they can do. In 80 percent of cases, when I ask someone to do something (that is a good use of their time and skills), they are happy to do it. This builds their sense of validation and belonging.

As an example, I used to run a community around an audio application called Jokosher. We had three new members join, and I asked them to work on specific documentation. In another project I asked community members to contribute a set of tests for assuring the quality of some mobile applications. In each of these cases these members did great work and were happy to be asked to be involved.

Regular: The key with Regulars is to *remove any and all frustration and bureaucracy from their participation.* Keep them focused on efficiently consuming and creating value. Think of your community like a workplace. The workplaces we love are ones that are simple, collaborative, and efficient. The workplaces we detest have layers upon layers of complexity, approvals, reviews, and other bureaucracy.

There are five things to focus on when engaging with Regulars:

1. *Optimize, Optimize, Optimize.* Always observe how your Regulars are engaging and find ways to make it easier, more efficient, and

more fun. Watch how they work, try to spot problems, and understand the problem spots. How can your guidelines be simplified? How can your tools be easier to use? How can you help their work be more rewarding? Always strive to refine these areas.

2. *Regularly gather their feedback.* Build a close relationship with your Regulars and ask them which elements of the community could be improved. Gather their feedback, make changes, and thank them for helping to improve the overall experience for everyone. Think of your Regulars as being on your team: they can provide insight into your blind spots.

3. *Promote their successes.* Your Regulars provide a backbone of contributions in your community. Celebrate them in your content plan, social media, events, and beyond. Make them into mini celebrities that everyone knows and respects. This validation will keep them coming back to participate and encourage others to do the same.

4. *Provide opportunities.* Always be on the lookout for opportunities you can offer to your Regulars. Are they looking for a new job? See if you can connect them to career opportunities you are aware of. Can you invite them to your organization's events or meetings? Can you send them to a conference to represent the community? The more opportunities you open for your Regulars, the better. It will help them to feel part of the team.

5. *Put them in positions of trust and authority.* Many of your Regulars will be people you can trust. Put these people in positions of authority in the community. Make them moderators on your communication channels, have them in positions of reviewing and publishing content, invite them to manage infrastructure or run

events. *If they are dependable, start to depend on them.* It will spread the load on your team and give these Regulars a renewed sense of belonging.

Core: These folks don't just care about their own community experience; they care about the broader health and success of the community itself. They care about your on-ramps, how you incentivize people, how your community communicates and engages with each other and more. They are the kind of people organizations would (and do) hire in a heartbeat.

There are five key things you should do with all your Core members:

1. *Have a regular engagement with them.* These are the people you engage with on a weekly basis. Schedule a regular call. Build personal friendships. Regularly ask them for guidance and celebrate the great work they do.

2. *Reward them comprehensively.* Invite them to invitation-only dinners with you, the leadership team, and others. Send them gifts and swag as a token of appreciation. Send them personalized mementos such as plaques, trophies, and challenge coins. Provide recognition of their work in your community and beyond. All of this helps to reaffirm your appreciation for their participation and devotion.

3. *Include them at a strategic level.* Your Core members have tremendous insight. Bring them into company meetings about existing and new initiatives (under the understanding that they keep the discussions in confidence). Get their feedback, ask them to suggest blind spots and flaws, and invite them to help you improve and refine the overall community experience. Again, consider them extended members of your team.

4. *Understand and serve their broader goals.* Try to understand what their broader ambitions and goals are, and serve them as best you can. This could include making introductions, writing testimonials for them, and suggesting them for speaking gigs at events. Again, your servitude to their goals furthers their trust and participation.

5. *Invite blunt feedback.* Finally, no matter how much you invite feedback from your community, some people just won't be comfortable being blunt or critical. *The most likely people to provide this feedback are your Core members.* They will feel comfortable enough in their community standing that they believe blunt feedback won't limit them and will be welcomed. Be direct in specifically requesting critical feedback to help you improve the overall community experience.

The Power of Mentoring

One morning, after a rough night's sleep thanks to the jet lag that kept on giving, I walked over to the head office of a large electronics manufacturer based in Tokyo. We started a week of community strategy meetings.

This company had ambitious ideas. They wanted a volunteer community of five thousand engineers in the next few years, but they had only a small tiger-team of five staff working on the project. With a goal of five thousand members, how on earth would five people be able to manage and engage them? Was I really expecting each staff member to manage one thousand people?

Yes.

Just kidding. Of course not; that would be nuts. The solution to this problem was to build a foundation of clear mentoring and peer-to-peer support. One of the benefits of the segmentation in the Community Participation Framework is that we can build predictable relationships between each phase.

Grabbing my marker to scribble some arrows down, I showed them that this is our goal:

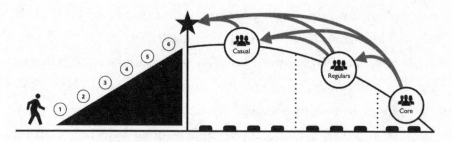
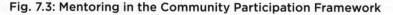

Fig. 7.3: Mentoring in the Community Participation Framework

The only way you can build a community that scales up is to help your community to help each other. You do this by encouraging members further along their community journey to provide mentoring and peer support to newer members.

Imagine someone is progressing up the on-ramp for the first time. You don't just want Casual members to help them, but also Regulars, and Core members. When Casual members are just getting going, you want Regulars and Core members to help them too. Similarly, when Regulars are facing some tricky challenges, you want Core members to help unstick them. *Mentoring builds a culture that "pays it forward."*

There are three approaches to mentoring, all which can add incredible value.

1. *Peer-Based Review.* Peer-based review is when community members review and provide feedback on the work of other members.

Peer review is one of the most powerful ways of scaling out how your members provide actionable feedback to other members. A good example of this is how code is often reviewed in open-source projects.

Without delving too deep into nerd land, engineering communities typically collaborate around code when a community member submits a pull request to a project. This is a chunk of code that can be applied to an existing set of code in different places. It is like a Band-Aid that adds additional functionality.

In open-source communities such as Kubernetes, Drupal, and jQuery, pull requests are typically submitted publicly. Then other developers go in and review that pull request and provide feedback, also out in the open. They may request it to be modified or improved, or they may say that it looks great! When the pull request is considered approved, one or more developers will mark it as approved and then it will be merged into the main codebase.

This is powerful for a number of reasons. First, *anyone and everyone is welcome to submit a pull request.* This provides a great opportunity for new developers, students, teenagers, and others to cut their teeth getting involved in a community. Second, *this feedback is an essential part of the learning process* for community members and always improves the overall quality of the code. Third, because this happens out in the open, *everyone can benefit from seeing the feedback,* even if they are simply an observer, thus building a history of how the project was built. Finally, it provides a way to *allow hundreds of contributions to be reviewed without bogging down a small set of approvers.*

Take a look at your audience personas and see how this can be applied to the methods of collaboration you may be focused on. *Can you have people peer-review documentation, videos, support material, advocacy materials, or other types of content that your community produces?* In many cases the answer to this question is yes. You just need a simple workflow for doing so, and it provides a great way of providing solid mentoring.

2. *Coaching*: Another method of mentoring is for a member to provide broader coaching to another member based on their goals. This is typically much more involved than peer-based review.

I usually recommend this in handpicked scenarios. When I have done this before, at any one time I would identify three to five people who I thought showed notable potential in the community. For example, they may be Regulars who could potentially become Core members.

I then identify members who I know can provide high-quality coaching (preferably with prior experience teaching/training) and ask them if they would be open to mentoring those members. If they agree, I connect them and encourage them to:

- Put in place a clear set of short-term goals (e.g., specific pieces of work).
- Provide recommendations for further skills development and training. This could be hands-on training or pointing them to other resources.
- Have weekly calls to help the mentee accomplish those goals, solve problems, and build their confidence and capabilities.

The tricky thing with coaching is that there are always significantly more people who need coaching than mentors available. As such, apply these coaches carefully and to the folks with the most potential.

For many people, mentoring others is fun and rewarding. If you think someone could be a good mentor, whether a staff member or community volunteer, ask them. You may be surprised just how many people are happy to help.

3. *Training*: The third and final type of mentoring is more general in nature: *training*.

Training is useful to train groups of people in developing specific sets of skills and experience. This provides a great way to impact lots of people, but it lacks the personal touch of the previous two types of mentoring.

As a general rule, you should run one or two training sessions a quarter that cover the most critical knowledge gaps in your community. These can be run as online webinars and usually are not longer than an hour in length. We will cover how to do this in more depth in chapter 9.

Look at the areas where you strategically want to build skills and capabilities and where there is interest. Now produce those training sessions and encourage people to join. Make them hands-on and dynamic, not just a boring slide deck. Make them interactive. Allow people to ask questions and request certain things to be demoed to answer their queries. This can be hugely valuable in increasing your communities' capabilities.

OBSERVE, HYPOTHESIZE, EXPERIMENT

As you put the recommendations in this book into action, you should monitor how well they perform. Capture data, review it, and look for patterns. These patterns will not just help you optimize that specific activity but also build skills in your organization for always refining and optimizing your strategy. This is how you build competence.

You can do this by following five steps, illustrated with an example that is threaded through each:

Step 1. Observe the data and look for patterns. As with everything you do, measure the performance of that work, evaluate it, and try to spot patterns that either point to problems or potential.

Example: Imagine you have published your content plan for a few months (focused on an Engineering persona), and you have noticed that shorter blog posts seem to get a higher rate of hits as well as a better bounce rate.

Step 2. Develop a hypothesis. When you spot a pattern, develop a hypothesis that you would like to test. For example, if you notice an increase in traffic given certain conditions, is it worth testing those conditions? Are there types of content, engagement, or events that seem to perform better and are worth testing?

Example: Based on the data, we suspect shorter blog posts are performing better than longer ones. We want to (a) see if this hypothesis is true, and (b) see what impact the length of an article has on readership.

Step 3. Devise an experiment. Based on your hypothesis, develop a simple, cheap experiment you can run to test it. This should run for a short period of time and generate enough data to prove or disprove your hypothesis.

As a general rule, every experiment you design should include (a) your hypothesis, (b) how you will test it, (c) the duration of the experiment, and—importantly—(d) which changes you will make if the hypothesis is either proven or disproven. *Never run an experiment that you can't map to actionable changes in your community.*

Example: To test the short-blog-post hypothesis, we will distribute six blog posts over the coming weeks, all technical in nature (so for the same Engineering persona). Two of these posts will be 150 words long, two will be 300 words long, and two will be 1000 words long. We will promote these equally and track the number of hits, the bounce rate, and the reader rating for each post after it has been live for two weeks.

Step 4. Review the results. Review the data from your experiment. Did it provide any insight into whether your hypothesis was correct (or even had the opposite effect)? In some cases the data may be so jumbled that it does not provide concrete data either way. If so, it might be worth trying a different experiment to test the same hypothesis.

Example: When we look at the data from our blog-post-length experiment, we find that the shorter posts get on average 30 percent more reads and a 10 percent improvement in bounce rate. The longer posts performed the worst. This proves our hypothesis was true.

Step 5. Determine next steps. Based on the results of the experiment, review and amend your strategy. Again, *never test a hypothesis and then fail to make any strategic adjustments based on it.* Otherwise, all of this work is a waste of time.

Example: In this case, we will optimize our future content to be shorter in overall length. We will adjust our guidelines for authors who are producing content as part of our Editorial Calendar to revise the size of their articles. We will also track the performance of these posts over a longer period of time to ensure our hypothesis sticks.

STAY LASER FOCUSED ON CREATIVITY AND MOMENTUM

Creativity is a loaded, ambiguous notion. One person's creativity is another person's snooze-fest, but you are going to need a mountain of it to successfully tap into and build momentum in your target audience.

The world is fighting more than ever before for our attention. You understand the *value* you want to create. You know your *audience.* You know ways to build *growth* and *engage* with your audience. Now you need to come up with ideas that will both surprise and intrigue them.

Without wishing to sound like a raging cliché, think outside the box. The Firefox community made crop circles as part of their advocacy. They solicited donations from their fifty-thousand-strong community and put an ad in the *New York Times* where the logo was comprised of the names of the donors.[9] They thought bigger, and it grabbed people's attention.

The best ideas come from different brains, so get more brains involved in the process. You never know: you just might touch on something that electrifies your audience with excitement.

CHAPTER 8

Mobilize Your Community Army

Fortune befriends the bold.
—Emily Dickinson

Societies are fascinating to me. Just think about it: we as the human race, composed of more than 7 billion people, have become surprisingly organized in how we live. We have cordoned off the world into continents, then into countries, and further into local municipalities. We have wired up our communities with plumbing, electricity, and sanitation, which is becoming increasingly available around the world.

We have formed into governments, who have levied taxes and laws to fund and bring order to societies. While of course many of these governments and laws are imperfect, many work well. This has produced the opportunity for people to have a global footprint, to travel, to trade, and to understand the cultures of people on the other side of the planet.

Let us not forget, though, that we are animals. The animal kingdom isn't like Winnie the Pooh. It is a brutal, violent, kill-or-be-killed world. We have created these societies because humans have figured out how to produce a powerful mix of incentives and rewards, and these incentives have a fundamental impact on human behavior.

In a nutshell: when we map the right rewards to the right incentives, they can generate desirable human behavior, which in turn generates value. Fortunately, human beings respond well to incentives. We receive a salary for going to work, we shop at the same stores when we receive gifts for regular custom, we love to collect trophies in video games, and we respond well to cash bonuses, overtime pay, and other ways of getting something for giving something.

We are incentivized by status, such as being at the top of a leaderboard in a live spin class, speaking at a TEDx event, or getting the next job title up the chain. *We are incentivized by clear rewards, great experiences, working with smart people, and accomplishing new or novel outcomes.*

Here's the tricky thing though: crafting incentives is *hard*. While coming up with ideas for incentives can be a fun exercise for you and your team, wiring them up to work predictably is complicated. This can often result in expensive experiments that deliver limited results.

Let's go back to our familiar Community Participation Framework. It incorporates my approach to how we decide on and deliver these incentives.

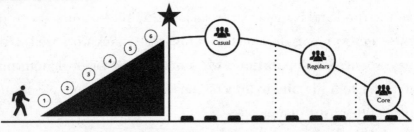

As you know by now, our goal is to keep our audience members progressing from the left to the right.

Incentives are the little dots at the bottom that present opportunities and rewards to the members who generate the desired behavior. You can look at each phase (Casual, Regulars, and Core) and design which types of incentives you need at that point in the journey to continue their growth and momentum.

These incentives should spur your members to produce tangible content, material, and skills. Importantly though, *you shouldn't just incentivize the things you can measure with computers but also the things you can measure only with judgement and observation from your community team,* such as good conduct, being trustworthy, providing care, and building belonging. In this chapter we get into what these incentives are, how we create them, and the value they can generate.

THE POWER OF INCENTIVIZATION

Incentives often appear simple on the surface, but there can be a lot of complexity under the covers. Let's first explore the anatomy of an incentive and then cover how to produce and distribute them.

The Anatomy of an Incentive

There are thousands of potential incentives you can apply to your community. It could be celebrating people who have participated regularly with public recognition and adoration. It could be sending someone a customized mug the first time they submit a new contribution to your knowledge base. It could be inviting someone to your office to participate in a leadership meeting.

Every incentive has three fundamental ingredients encased inside it.

1. *The Goal*: First, what is the desired behavior you want to incentivize? Do you want people to answer questions, write code, run events, or something else?

Look at your audience personas, your Big Rocks, and what you want members to accomplish. Prioritize the most critical types of participation. This will provide a list of the goals for each incentive you create.

As you think about each goal, think about how you measure if it has been accomplished. Kick ambiguity to the curb. Be specific: what measurable outcome signals that the goal has been achieved?

2. *The Reward*. Go back to your audience personas and look at the Motivations section. What kind of rewards and recognition motivates them? This will vary tremendously depending on your personas.

There are two broad categories of rewards to consider here.

Extrinsic. These are material things we know and love such as T-shirts, stickers, and gadgets. Think outside the box and be thoughtful. HackerOne made superhero comic book covers of their top contributors.[1] Mattermost gave their Regular community members customized mugs.[2] Buffer would tune their swag to the individual (such as sending dog chew sticks and a note to a known canine fan).[3]

Intrinsic. These rewards thank someone for doing great work and gives them a sense of personal satisfaction and belonging. Celebrate great work from your members on websites, blogs, and social media. Invite Regular and Core members to dinners with your team. Provide Core members with a direct line to your leadership.

When designing your rewards, always *start with intrinsic rewards first.* This may seem counterintuitive, but intrinsic rewards will almost always have a positive impact whereas extrinsic rewards run the risk of having a moment of novelty value that is then forgotten. We will cover this more later in the chapter.

Intrinsic rewards build satisfaction and belonging. Think carefully about how you can beef up someone's self-confidence and satisfaction in the community. It is incredible the impact a simple personal email thanking someone can have, as well as recognizing them in a public place such as a blog, video, or event.

Be careful with extrinsic rewards. It is easy to default to the tried-and-tested extrinsic rewards, and company after company schleps T-shirts, stickers, and other tat to their community members. Most critically, *make your swag meaningful and personal.* Include a personal, handwritten note as a bare minimum.

Also, be careful with how much you reward people. Inspired by the Yerkes Dodson scale, which covers the link between arousal and performance,[4] I have noticed a similar trend between performance of participants in communities and the distribution of rewards, as outlined by my Participant Rewards Peak shown in figure 8.1:

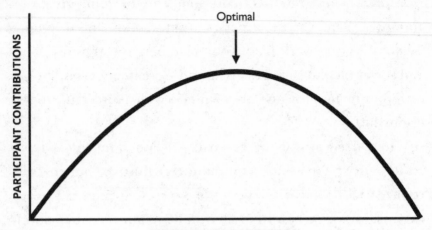

Fig. 8.1: Participant Rewards Peak

In a nutshell, if you distribute the right balance of rewards based on performance you can incentivize peak results. There is a risk though of oversupplying rewards to the point where the participant is so focused on getting the rewards that their priority becomes the rewards and not doing great work. Be careful not to overdo the extrinsic rewards and always monitor the balance of performance compared to the rewards you provide to see if this is happening.

3. *The Condition*: The final piece of the puzzle is the condition. That is, what measurable criteria needs to be met to accomplish the reward?

The idea is simple: we want to plumb this criterion into our community so that when it is triggered, it generates the reward with the most limited amount of manual attention.

There are four considerations in deciding on your condition:

1. *Be Measurable.* First, as a general rule the condition needs to be objectively measurable. Can you assess whether the condition was accomplished with a "yes" or "no"? Again, there are no "maybes" in our lexicon here. "Answer twenty questions" is measurable, but "Be a devoted question-answerer" is not. *Get specific. Stay specific.*

The exception here is with rewarding general human behavior (e.g., mentorship, insight, kindness, and support). In these cases, you need to observe this behavior, so be clear on what you want to measure and ensure others share your definition of what "good" is.

2. *Be Representative.* Does this condition represent the behavior you want to see? For example, if you want to encourage your community to provide help, merely posting to a forum isn't necessarily a good measure of quality. What we really want to see is high-quality content, so maybe an approval (or even a simple "like") is a better way of judging this behavior. As we discussed earlier, when you lay out incentives, it will change behavior, and some folks will abuse the system to accomplish the reward. Ensure your condition can avoid these bottom-dwellers by providing safeguards to reduce abuse (such as entrance criteria or requiring approval/validation).

3. *Be Varied in Difficulty.* You should gauge how difficult it is to accomplish this condition. Your incentives shouldn't all be SEAL team training missions; they should provide a wide range of incentives at different difficulties. Fortunately, we can use our Casual, Regular, and Core segments to guide us. We will cover this more a little later in this chapter.

4. *(Where Possible) Be Automated.* Where possible, measure your condition with a computer and react to those measurements. This

can be a single metric or combination of metrics. Always be clear what these measurements should identify. For example, detecting when a code submission has been approved, a question has been answered, or a member has answered their tenth question in one month (to detect consistent participation).

As I mentioned earlier, some behaviors are difficult to measure with a computer, such as social development and interaction. In those cases, ensure that your team is clear on what success looks like, and depend on them to observe and react when they see it.

INCENTIVES: TWO GREAT FLAVORS

OK, we have a good idea of the value of incentives and the constituent parts. How do you produce an incentive strategy?

Our fundamental goal is to plot a series of incentives that keep people transitioning forward, first to the on-ramp, then to Casual, on to Regular, and then to Core. Strategically, you should build your first set of incentives at the transition points between these phases, illustrated by my Incentive Transition Points in figure 8.2:

🚶 O▸ On-Ramp O▸ Casual O▸ Regular O▸ Core

Fig. 8.2: Incentive Transition Points

These transition points are when community members are at the greatest risk of getting distracted by that new Netflix show and falling away. For example, how do you incentivize someone to get on the on-ramp for the first time? A simple solution here could be rewarding them when they produce that first piece of value at the end of the on-ramp (many organizations reward this accomplishment with validation and/or a gift).

How do you transition this first accomplishment into Casual participation? Here you should incentivize repeated participation, such as rewards for developing new skills, producing new material, and supporting the success of others.

For the transition to the Regular phase, incentivize and reward when people step up to the plate with additional responsibility. Importantly, in this phase you should explore ways community members can take the initiative and play more and more of a leadership role.

In chapter 1, I quoted Emmy Award–winner Joseph Gordon-Levitt, who shared with me the importance of leadership, not just in the creative process but in the formation of his HITRECORD community. "An open collaborative process really needs leadership. This is a big part of how we've built our platform and community. At first it was always me leading our collaborative projects, but over the years, it's been great to see members of the community step into those leadership roles themselves."[5]

The Regular phase is an opportunity to identify these leaders. Provide lightweight opportunities for members to lead, mentor, and use their initiative.

Finally, for the transition to the Core phase, produce a narrower but deeply valuable set of personal incentives for particularly outstanding leadership and devotion. Incentivize them for helping to shape new initiatives, solve tough problems, improve key elements of the community, etc.

To design and deliver these kinds of incentives, I break them down into two primary categories.

Stated incentives are clearly communicated opportunities for community members to participate in. They are published and have clear criteria and rewards. Stated incentives include gamification badges, competitions, hackathons, and contests. They are similar to quests in video games: if you accomplish an outcome, you receive some kind of reward, even if it is just a badge or virtual trophy.

Submarine incentives are the sneaky cousin to stated incentives. They are preprogrammed ways in which we can detect great community participation and then validate and reward it in a human, personal way. They appear like seemingly random acts of kindness—the random gifts you receive for doing something, the kind email from the founder of a project supporting your recent work, and the opportunities that open up the more you participate.

Both of these types of incentives are enormously valuable in a community. Let's delve into each in more detail and how we produce them.

Stated Incentives

If you peel open any modern video game, particularly multiplayer and open-world games, you find a delicately crafted set of incentives. For example, many first-person-shooters award points at the end of each round, which can then be spent on equipment, weapons, and more. These points are distributed based on how well you played, and it incentivizes players to improve their skills.

Stated incentives are *clearly communicated up front.* You can window-shop for rewards and get them if you accomplish the stated goal.

Take a look at the transition points in figure 8.2 and produce five to ten incentives spread across these transition points. Here are some examples (each of these would be promoted openly as incentives and their associated rewards):

On-Ramp

- If a member answers their first question in a support forum, they receive a badge that is visible in their member profile.
- If a member contributes their first piece of (approved) content to a blog, they earn a free e-book with writing best practices (useful for future work).
- If the member gets their first app approved for a platform they get a "care kit" with T-shirt, cap, free training materials, and the name of the app etched into a statue outside the company office.

On-Ramp → Casual

- If a member has ten of their responses to other members' questions accepted as answers, they are sent a personal note and a ten-dollar gift card to an online store.
- If the member has five of their code contributions reviewed and approved, they get highlighted in a blog post in the community.

Casual → Regular

- Launch an online hackathon to see who can fix the greatest number of bugs in the community project in one week. The first-, second-, and third-place winners will receive prizes, and everyone who submits a bug that is fixed will be highlighted in an article and on the website.

- A content contest is launched to produce the best tutorial videos for a product. The top three videos (based on a judging panel's votes) win a specific set of prizes.

Regular → Core

- Members who get voted onto a community leadership board will have direct email access to the company leadership team.
- The top ten ranking members in terms of reputation will be invited out to three days of meetings at the organization's headquarters, with full travel, board, and meals provided.

Think also about empowering your community members to reward people. A previous client had a system where employees had a limited amount of cash each month (sixty-five dollars) that they could use to reward other employees via spot cash rewards. As an example, a designer did a great job for a product manager, and she gave him ten dollars from her sixty-five-dollar budget. Interestingly, the employees who made the most money were the front desk, receptionist, and admin staff (arguably, the most under-appreciated people in a company).

These rewards were popular, not just for those receiving the money but also for how it empowered the staff to distribute them.

Submarine Incentives

As we discussed in the last chapter, one of the major challenges as communities grow is in maintaining a *personal* touch. For small communities of less than 150 people, this is less of an issue because you and your team can engage with your members directly. As you grow larger though, it can be difficult to maintain this personal touch. There are simply too many people to keep track of.

Submarine incentives are one tool for dealing with this problem. They are *preprogrammed incentives and rewards that, when triggered, provide an opportunity for us to engage personally with a member.* This allows us to scale up and still be personal.

As one example, a previous client had a web platform. When one of their users submitted content via their platform, we would award points based on the quality of the content. We would then use these reputation points to deliver a series of incentives and rewards.

One such reward was when a user submitted around five pieces of content (which demonstrated a repeated level of participation in the platform). The system would detect the fifth submission, notify us, and we would send them a personal email offering to send them a T-shirt. This wasn't a published "If you submit five high-quality submissions you get a shirt" incentive. They simply got an email out of the blue from someone saying:

> Hi Sarah,
>
> I just noticed you have been doing some really amazing work in our community recently, and I saw the flurry of high-quality submissions. I was particularly impressed with your most recent contribution and how you [. . .]
>
> I would love to send you a T-shirt as a sign of our appreciation. Please go and fill in this form with your shipping address and size.

Also, if you have any questions, or I can help with anything, just let me know; you have my email address now.

Joe

Importantly, *this email wasn't sent from a robotic email address; it was sent from a real person at the company.* It was written by a real human being. Sure, the system detected when the incentive was triggered, but the offer of help was very real and tuned to the recipient, and this built a personal connection with the community member.

Again, get creative with this. One community I worked with detected when it was a Regular or Core member's birthday and sent them a nice note. Another community detected when a community member's first contribution was not approved, and they would send them some recommendations and a free e-book to help. *Use a computer to detect, but ask a person to engage.*

Noah Everett is the founder of Twitpic, which at its peak had 30 million users and eighty thousand joining every day.[6] He shared with me the importance of this personal touch. "Be very proactive in talking and interacting with those in your community. Try to respond quickly and be sincere. Take the time to craft your response to make it personal (i.e., use their name or reference something they wrote previously) so they know you are actually paying attention and care." He summarized it simply, "Being authentic is one of, if not the most important, DOs for communicating online."[7]

Submarine incentives are particularly powerful for delivering personal validation (an *intrinsic* reward). In another company, when a member earned their way into the Top 100 users, we would send them an email informing them that they were added to a special category of users and provided with direct access to the executive team via a special email address.

This provided another important psychological function of elevated *status* and *access*. While they rarely used this email address, the members appreciated that it was there if needed. Everyone needs a bat phone sometimes.

When considering submarine incentives, there are a few important rules to follow:

1. *Make them fair.* As with all incentives, you need to make these fair. People will share and discuss them with others, and when they do, you want to ensure that they objectively earned the reward. You should avoid the perception they were rewarded with something when they didn't really earn it.

2. *Keep the recipe secret.* While you should keep submarine incentives secret, some people will discover them. In these cases, it is fine to acknowledge that your community is filled with little incentives, but *never give the recipe for how to accomplish them away*. It will shatter the surprise and people will game the system so they can accomplish the reward.

3. *Mix extrinsic and intrinsic rewards.* As we discussed earlier, submarine incentives are particularly powerful for providing validation and appreciation. They can be used for delivering extrinsic material rewards such as T-shirts, mugs, trophies, and more. Be careful though in estimating the right number of these rewards so your budgets don't balloon out of control.

4. *Make them personal.* Never ever have the communication with the member be a prewritten form email or notification. *Computers should detect patterns, but humans should do the communicating.* If you

don't do this, you run the risk of making your members feel tricked, just like those awful robocalls for Las Vegas getaways that pretend to be a real person.

5. *Build in access and engagement.* As people go further and further through the phases we discussed earlier (Casual, Regular, and Core), provide them with more and more access to the leadership and company. Use submarine incentives to trigger opportunities for access and influence. For example, with one client I had a submarine incentive trigger when a major contribution was made, and the CEO would personally call the member to thank them. This is *remarkably* powerful.

6. *Start small and build up.* Don't overdo it. Generate five to ten submarine incentives spread across the phases we discussed earlier. See which ones work and which ones don't. Then build up from there. Here are some examples at our different transition points. Remember these would not be publicly stated. They would trigger and generate surprise rewards for members.

On-Ramp

- If a submitted contribution is accepted (e.g., content, code), they are emailed a personal thank-you from the community leader.
- If a submitted contribution is rejected, an email is sent with recommendations for improvements and next steps with links to articles and support resources.

On-Ramp → Casual

- When a member has submitted five answers to questions that are submitted, they receive a personal email from the community leader, thanking them.

- When a member contributes an article that gets the highest number of hits in a month, they are sent a twenty-five dollar gift voucher to an online store and are highlighted in a monthly blog (about great work and content).
- If 70 percent of the bugs a member has submitted for a product are valid reports, they are invited to join private testing of the software (with early access).

Casual → Regular

- When a member has submitted twenty-five answers that are accepted, they are sent a "community rock star" challenge coin.
- If a member contributes a new feature that is included in the next release, they are highlighted in a blog post and are sent a limited-edition T-shirt that highlights them as a developer.
- When a member has contributed thirty pieces of content (e.g., articles), they are sent a personal email inviting them to the office to have coffee with the team (and get some swag) if they are ever in town.

Regular → Core

- When a member accomplishes a notable milestone (such as their five-hundredth contribution), they get a call from the CEO of your company.
- The top five members in your community (based on reputation) are sent personal invitations to join the leadership team in the community and the company for strategic meetings, dinner, and drinks (with travel and accommodation covered).

DOING "REPUTATION" WELL

Before we get onto how to build our incentives strategy, I want to touch on reputation. Reputation is commonly a numerical representation of an individual member's participation in your community. It is the shadow of their character and participation. Reddit calls it *karma*. Nintendo calls it *points*. Discourse calls it *trust levels*. Battlefield calls it *kills* (of course).

As an example, Reddit karma is awarded for popular links and comments shared by their members.[8] Like Reddit, most communities keep the algorithm for how they calculate their reputation scores secret, even if the total number itself is public.

One client I worked with would provide ten points for good work submitted, zero points for a terrible piece of work submitted, and a graduation based on this scale. As such, five points was OK, seven was good, and ten was excellent. Of course, the grading on this was subjective, but no reputation system is perfect. You have to design it to be as effective as possible. This score should preferably be calculated automatically.

Importantly, *reputation should decay over time.* The goal of a reputation score is to not just grade individual contributions, but to provide a total score that reflects which community members are doing great work *around this time.* If they stop participating, you should decay the score gradually. As an example, you may want to decay 1 percent of the total score every two weeks in which activity falls below a specific threshold.

This will ensure that reputation is a current figure as opposed to an historical one. If you don't decay reputation, people who join your community earlier will always have an unfair advantage; newcomers won't be able to catch up. Of course, if you decay your reputation, be sure to do it gradually. For example, don't penalize mothers who take time off to have a kiddo.

If you do calculate a reputation score, it can be a fantastically useful metric for (a) seeing the spread of the least to most active members, (b) spotting trends in activity, (c) determining how your users are divided across our Casual, Regular, and Core phases, and (d) providing a Condition (that we discussed earlier) for your incentives and rewards.

Think carefully if you should publish your member reputation scores. If you have a community that is designed to be competitive in nature (such as a game), it might make a lot of sense to publish it. If your community is more collaborative in nature (such as an Inner Collaborator community), you might not want to. While status is a powerful incentive for some, others can feel disillusioned that they "don't measure up." Gather feedback from people in your community and organization before you make this decision.

BUILD AN INCENTIVES MAP

An incentives map is a clearly articulated and stated plan for which incentives we are going to plumb into our community throughout the different phases we outlined earlier. It is similar to our Quarterly Delivery Plan but designed to pull together your target incentives. It looks like this:

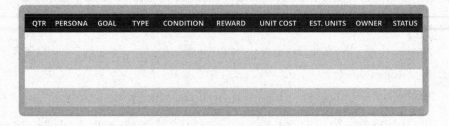

QTR	PERSONA	GOAL	TYPE	CONDITION	REWARD	UNIT COST	EST. UNITS	OWNER	STATUS

Fig. 8.3: Incentives Map Template

Here's how it works:

Quarter: As with the items in our Quarterly Delivery Plan, it is essential that you clearly understand when each of these incentives should be in place and available. Add the target quarter here. For some *stated* incentives that are individual initiatives (such as a competition), this is particularly important.

Persona: Add which of your target personas this incentive is focused on. Make sure all personas have incentives for every transition point outlined in figure 8.2.

Goal: Now add the behavioral goal you have for this incentive. For example, this could be "Make a first contribution," or "Providing mentoring to members."

Type: Add the type of incentive this is (stated or submarine) so you can ensure you have the right balance of both.

Condition: Now add the measurable condition for this incentive. Remember our golden rules earlier: this needs to be *measurable, representative, automated,* and with a clear level of *difficulty* represented by the phase it is in (Casual, Regular, or Core).

Reward(s): Now outline the intrinsic (e.g., validation, thanks) and/or extrinsic (e.g., swag, gift cards) reward that will be delivered for this incentive.

Unit Cost. If you are delivering an extrinsic reward, add the individual unit cost for that reward (including average shipping and handling). This will be helpful for calculating budgets.

Estimated Units: Again, for extrinsic rewards, add the estimated number of units you expect to ship each quarter. Again, this is useful for determining overall budgets.

Owner: Just like with our Quarterly Delivery Plan, every incentive needs an owner. This individual is responsible for the overall delivery of the incentive. This includes provisioning the rewards, ensuring the condition can be detected in an automated way, and handling how the member is notified of any rewards they have earned.

Status: Finally, just like our Quarterly Delivery Plan, track the current status of how far along the incentive is going from idea to implementation. I recommend you use the similar statuses we covered in chapter 5: Not Started, In Progress, Under Review, Available To Members, Delayed, Blocked, and Postponed.

Here is an example of a stated and submarine incentive:

Quarter	Q2
Persona	Support
Goal	Providing support to community members
Type	Submarine
Condition	Member has a registered account on the forum
	Member answers a question from another user
	Question submitter marks the answer as solving the problem

Reward(s)	Personal email from Head of Community thanking them Copy of an e-book
Unit Cost	$2 (e-book)
Est. Units	80
Owner	Sarah Jones
Status	In Progress
Quarter	Q2
Persona	Developer
Goal	Contributing first new feature to the project
Type	Stated
Condition	First code branch is merged into the project
Reward(s)	Thanks email from engineering lead
Unit Cost	$0
Est. Units	50
Owner	Dave Rogers
Status	Available to Members

GAMIFICATION

A while back I was at an Ubuntu Developer Summit in Europe and a few colleagues and I were bouncing around the idea of some kind of gamification system for Ubuntu. The idea was simple: when people participated in Ubuntu in different ways, we would provide them with badges that they could collect. As with all simple ideas, there was a lot of complexity buried under the surface.

My experiment specifically focused on the development of new skills. It covered a wide range of methods of participation, including engineering, governance, support, documentation, and more. It presented a set of available badges (some of which needed to be earned before others), and community members could discover them, learn how to accomplish them, and then get started.[9]

My system was popular, but it also made some people nervous; they worried that it would generate "inauthentic participation"— that is, not participating to make Ubuntu better, but instead just to get the badge. This taught me a lot about striking the right balance of incentives and communal collaboration. Out of this work, and studying gamification in other communities (e.g., multiplayer games, exercise groups, and others), I recommend you follow a key set of rules.

1. First, *focus on onboarding and skills acquisition.* For example, you could gamify setting up a new profile, producing a first piece of content, answering your first question, running your first event, or something else. Don't gamify based on repetition of activity (e.g., tenth post, one hundredth post, one thousandth post) as this can be easily abused.

2. As you design your gamification platform, *discovery is critical.* Peloton promotes new challenges when you turn on the screen. Discourse has badges integrated into user profiles. PlayStation has trophies on the main screen. Make it simple for your community members to see what gamification opportunities are available, step-by-step instructions for how to accomplish them, where they can get help in doing so, and any other information.

3. *Gamification needs a clear path forward.* When you design a gamification system, it is easy to find dependencies. For example, if you want to gamify someone submitting an idea in a community for the first time, you may want to first gamify them registering an account. This way you can only make the idea-filing badge available if the registration badge is already accomplished. This provides a clear, logical path forward for the order these tasks can be accomplished.

4. As you do this work, *set clear expectations.* Provide simple, step-by-step instructions for what the member needs to do to accomplish the reward.

5. Be sure to *protect against "gaming the system."* With every game produced since the beginning of time, there have been people who want to break the rules and find shortcuts. You may not think people in your community will do this, but they will. Ensure that people can't trick your system into giving them rewards and put in place verification (either automated or manual) to ensure they have properly earned these rewards. Regularly invite people you trust to try gaming the system to see if they can abuse it (so you can fix the flaw).

6. Throughout this, *be careful of elevated egos.* Some people get crazy when they start collecting lots of rewards (such as badges), especially if those rewards are publicly visible. You should always ensure that your messaging and engagement makes it clear that gamification is one way of participating, but there are many other ways in which people add value. Sometimes you will need to perform an *ego calibration*, when you sit down with someone privately and ask them to tone it down a little bit. This is rare but sometimes needed.

Which Tech?

There are many different technology platforms and systems out there for accomplishing gamification. I am not highlighting specific ones in this book because (a) your needs may be different, and (b) technology moves faster than books, so the recommendations will be outdated quickly. Do some research, and if you get stuck, drop me an email: jono@jonobacon.com.

MAINTAIN THE PERSONAL TOUCH

Incentives are a powerful way to keep your members interested, engaged, and rewarded. Importantly though, always keep the *personal touch* front and center as you do this work. Communities thrive on personal relationships. People don't want to feel they are on a hamster wheel. They don't want to feel played. Incentives run the risk of coming across as systemic and contrived *if* you fail to properly use them as a means to foster, recognize, and build these relationships.

Look at your incentives through a cynical eye: have you struck the right balance? If not, refine them until they feel supportive of your members' success, validation, and relationships.

CHAPTER 9

Cyberspace and Meatspace:
Better Together

We all have a gift; we all have a passion—it's just about finding it and going into it. Being an asset to your family and community.
—Angela Bassett

As technology marches forward, more and more communities are not just going digital but becoming *primarily* digital. Given this, it is easy to think of in-person events and engagement as "nice to have" instead of essential. This is an enormous mistake.

While digital environments allow us to scale, they largely lack the presence and personality of in-person events and engagement. Working together in the same room builds relationships and trust and often results in more focused and efficient collaboration. If you ignore bringing your community together in-person in your strategy, you are missing out.

Here's the deal though: events can be expensive and time-consuming. If you don't manage them well, you will see large chunks of budget disappearing with little to show for it. We can unlock these benefits *if* we are strategic and focused in how we integrate in-person engagement into our overall strategy and ensure the digital and in-person realms are clearly connected.

CHARTING A REALISTIC EVENTS STRATEGY

When many of my clients start seeing some traction in their product or service, there is a temptation to start running their own events and conferences. *Many organizations don't realize how much work is involved in delivering a solid event,* and this can result in poor quality, underresourced events, with limited value.

Just like a small child, a small company or community needs to learn to walk before it can run. This is illustrated by my Event Evolution Path:

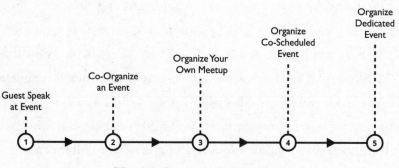

Fig. 9.1: Event Evolution Path

Start by *offering yourself as a guest speaker* at meetups or conferences. This requires a limited level of investment, and gets you in front of an audience. Don't make this a product or commercial pitch. *Focus on sharing lessons learned that are of general interest to the audience.* Practice, stay on time, and do a good job. This will get you invited to other events. Keep doing this at as many different-yet-relevant events and audiences as you can get in front of.

Now *co-organize a small event* (such as a meetup) with another organization. For example, the SCORECast film music community runs an annual meetup at the NAMM music show in Anaheim, California.[1] Keep things simple and focus on high-quality content. Provide a few talks, some Q&A, and plenty of networking. Provide drinks and tasty (and mostly healthy) food. Advertise the event extensively in the area, put posters up, promote it on social media, and generate a great turnout. Rinse and repeat a few more times.

As your community grows, it is time to *organize your own meetup.* Repeat the approach in the previous phase, but bigger and better. Have more in-depth content, have solid (and preferably well-known) speakers, and better food, drinks, and networking. *Free events can experience up to a 50 percent dropout rate, so go gangbusters in getting bums on seats.*

Now move toward *organizing a more in-depth, dedicated event* that is coscheduled next to another conference (so people are in town already). As an example, I run the Community Leadership Summit next to a large open-source conference.[2] This is where you will likely have many more attendees, multiple speakers and/or tracks, sponsors, exhibitors, and more. Again, focus extensively on promotion: events that fail haven't been promoted enough (or are not interesting enough). Nail it on both counts.

Finally, the ultimate step is to *organize your own dedicated event.* At this point you should have a dependable audience and community that will be interested in attending. You *have* to make this a success: the reputation and attendance of the event will reflect on you, your reputation, and your community.

As a general rule, only proceed to each next step in the Event Evolution Path if you have completed the previous steps along the way. Part of the reason I designed the Event Evolution Path this way is to gradually build the skills, expertise, expectations, and knowledge of the bumps in the road. Don't skip over phases: you simply open yourself and your community up to more risk that way.

Also, remember not every community will need to reach the dizzy heights of organizing a dedicated event. Different communities will have different aspirations for events, and that is fine.

Let's now explore some different ways of engaging with communities in person.

PARTICIPATING IN AND SPEAKING AT CONFERENCES

As you build your community, you will need to get out to events to raise awareness, meet community members, develop partnerships and more.

Participating in these events can represent an enormous cost to an organization. It isn't just the cost of the tickets and travel, it is also the time spent getting there, attending, getting home, and often recovering from the weird flu you picked up while there. Events also cause email and work to get backed up, so the week after the event there is the obligatory "digging out of my email" period. Good times (not).

When you evaluate which events to attend, judge them on (a) whether your target audience personas are there, (b) if they are of strategic benefit, and (c) the cost/benefit analysis of what you aim to accomplish. There *should be a clear value outcome for joining.* It should not be, "Well, we kind of need to be there."

When you do settle on an event, you should focus on getting the maximum value out of it. Be sure to follow my Conference Checklist:

- *Focus on speaking and content delivery.* As a general rule, only attend events if you can speak there. This will provide an important opportunity to address an audience, and it will also lower your costs (as your ticket should be comped by the conference). If you can't speak at a conference (e.g., your submission wasn't picked), only attend conferences you can see direct value in.
- *Plan meetings and local opportunities in advance.* At least *two weeks before the event* you should take a look at the event, the keynotes, attendees, and companies and reach out to people of strategic interest to book meetings. People get busy at the show, so get them booked before you get there.
- *Prioritize the hallway track.* You want to maximize time with other attendees at the event. Don't waste time in sessions unless they are necessary. Spend your time in the hallway, at the expo, at the social events, and other places where people congregate. This is where conversations spring up, not in rooms where people quietly watch a slide deck.
- *Bring business and community overview cards.* Always have something you can give someone when they are interested

in talking more. At a minimum this should be your business card, but you should also produce some business card–sized cards that provide an overview of the community and the first three steps for getting involved. They will find this after the event mixed in with their business cards and it gives them the information they need to get started.

- *Network extensively, especially at the social events.* There is a misnomer that the evening events at conferences and meetups are primarily aimed for socializing and in some cases, getting rather drunk. As such, many people skip the evening events and focus on the daytime content.

- *The evening events are where relationships are often formed.* Sharing a mixture of work and personal discussion is how people break the ice, build trust, and seal the likelihood of another (more substantive) meeting. My business has been largely built on these relationships, forged in bars, restaurants, at lunches, and social events. Booze is not required, so don't worry if you don't drink.

- *Divide and conquer.* One problem I see all the time at conferences is when people who work for the same company spend large chunks of the day or evening huddled together. Break the clique and divide and conquer! If there are two of you at a conference and you spend most of your time together, you not only reduce the potential surface area you can cover for meeting people, but you also send a signal that engagement with you is off limits (as you are spending time together and not with others).

- *After the event, follow up with further meetings.* The major goal for any meeting is to continue the conversation at a later date if it was valuable for both parties. The problem is that many people get home from the event and forget to follow up, or lose the business card. When you get back, *follow up while the conversation is fresh in your minds*. Schedule more time with a call or in-person meeting, and ensure you go to the meeting with (a) a clear goal of what you want, and (b) a clear sense of what you can offer.

BUILDING SKILLS AND TRAINING

You, your community, and your organization are only as good as the skills that power them. You should always focus on building skills and capabilities in yourself, your team, and your community members. The broader the skills base, the greater capabilities your community will have to produce value.

There is a rich mine of material ripe for training your community such as marketing/advocacy methods, how to use different products/infrastructure, how to organize events/meetups, leadership training, conflict resolution, and more.

I prefer two different approaches both of which mitigate the boredom often associated with training: *digital training* and *training workshops*. Let's look at each.

Method 1: Digital Training

This is training that takes place online. *Schedule it as a one-hour webinar that people can register for to learn a specific topic or skill.*

Importantly, schedule this for a time that makes sense for your target audience. If this is a global audience, early morning Pacific American time is usually a good time (it captures most of the US and Europe).

CasinoCoin holds regular community Q&A and roadmap sessions.[3] I have delivered training videos on topics such as handling difficult people and avoidable career mistakes.[4] Adobe delivers Photoshop "Magic Minute" videos with quick tips and tricks.[5] *There are many creative ways to deliver education in an interesting way.*

Spend the first three quarters of the session performing the training. Throughout the session, provide a place where people can ask questions. As you run through the training, answer questions if they make sense in context. Try not to just display slides. *Provide demos and interactive examples where it makes sense.* Then in the last fifteen minutes answer any remaining questions.

When the session is complete, *make the recording available in your community* (and promote it extensively to your community as an important cornerstone piece of content).

Method 2: Training Workshops

When running in-person training be sure to schedule it at a date, time, and location where your target audience is available. Training sessions coscheduled with conferences are a great fit. Keep the class fairly small; ideally less than thirty people.

When promoting your workshop, make it clear what specific benefits attendees will get out of it. What skills will they learn? How can they apply and use these skills?

Break the training session into a series of different individual classes that cover a key topic. Each class should last no longer than forty-five minutes to one hour.

Teach the fundamentals for ten to twenty minutes, and ensure the audience has a good understanding. Then break the audience into a series of small groups and give them a task that relates to the content and a set amount of time to complete it. For example, if providing social media training, ask them to come up with a sample social media campaign.

Ensure that they have enough time to accomplish the task comfortably. After the time wraps up, ask each group to share their findings with the rest of the training group. This provides a way for everyone to benefit from the ideas, network with other attendees, and keep the blood flowing.

RUNNING A COMMUNITY SUMMIT

When I was at Canonical, we used to run an event called the Ubuntu Developer Summit every six months, for nearly ten years.[6] It attracted more than five hundred attendees each time and it took us to far flung places in Europe, the Americas, and beyond. It didn't just become a place where we made decisions, but it became a place where people ate together, drank together, formed friendships, and consoled each other through tough times. This is where I discovered the value of organizing a main community summit at least once a year.

My recommended format is simple. Have a series of short morning keynotes (designed to be inspirational), but the bulk of the event is in-person round-table discussion sessions where attendees provide training, discuss ideas, and make plans. These summits can be a great mixture of tutorial content as well as planning for new initiatives and projects.

Each session has a clear goal: *to either teach a specific skill or technique or to get a clear set of tasks or recommendations to be delivered in coming months.* For example, for the latter, if one session is about producing a newsletter for the community, the session should end with a list of tasks for putting the newsletter plan into action.

I have found this format to work well with a number of clients and their events. It provides a way for the community to (a) be strategically involved in the community, (b) get aligned on projects, and (c) grow and develop skills and relationships. Let's explore how we run one.

Step 1: Decide on a Structure

I am a big fan of short, sharp keynotes in the morning and the bulk of the event focused on practical discussion sessions. It keeps people active, involved, and participating. As such I recommend this structure:

- *Mornings*: Two to four keynotes that are fifteen minutes long (for delivering skills and education).
- *Afternoons*: Three to five discussion sessions that are forty-five minutes long, with a few thirty-minute breaks included.
- *Evenings*: At least one main social event and preferably a few more informal social events.

Start with an opening keynote on the first morning that explains the goals of the event, logistics, and provides some Q&A. Conclude the event with a summary of decisions made throughout the sessions so everyone can leave with a clear sense of next steps.

Step 2. Finalize Attendees and Content

The success of summits is dependent on productive, constructive discussions and next steps. This is fueled by having the right combination of community members and people from your organization.

For your first event, keep it simple and small. Less than twenty people can provide enormous value. Make sure everyone who is invited has earned a place due to their active participation. *You should only be inviting Regulars and Core members.* Invite people who have already proven their value, not just people with opinions. Future events can be open to everyone and have a much bigger audience, but your first few events should focus on quality rather than quantity.

Don't just make your decision on who to invite based on people you like. If someone adds value but they are often challenging you, your decisions, and your approach, they may be one of the most valuable participants. *We don't want an echo chamber. We want an environment that drives us forward with our eyes open.*

If you invite key community members to join, they are taking time from their schedules and jobs to participate. As such, *cover their expenses.* You don't need to be extravagant. Many sponsorships cover economy air, a reasonable daily stipend, and have people share rooms (if appropriate) in a budget hotel.

Now, invite people to submit topics for discussion, taking this approach:

1. *Publicize the target themes of the next year.* People need guardrails to ensure the sessions they submit are relevant to where the community and/or product/service is focused. Three months before the event, publish a blog post summarizing your ideas for Big Rocks and key target themes for the next year. This provides some important context for what people should submit session ideas on.

2. *Provide a place where people can submit session ideas.* This could be as simple as a form, or as complex as a paper submission system. Make sure you clarify that these are working discussion sessions, not presentations like a typical conference. Provide at least *three weeks* for submissions.

The kind of sessions you want to have should be focused on developing new skills and new initiatives and projects. For example, this could include adding new features to the community, starting new teams, refining leadership boards, optimizing on-ramps, refining incentives, running new competitions, improving diversity, and running local events. Anything we have discussed in this book would make great fodder for sessions.

3. *Select sessions and send guidance.* Select sessions that will offer the most value in the summit and meet the overall goals of the event. Publish the schedule so everyone in the community can see what will be discussed.

Send guidance for how session leaders should prepare for and run their session. I recommend you use my Summit Session Structure as shown in figure 9.2:

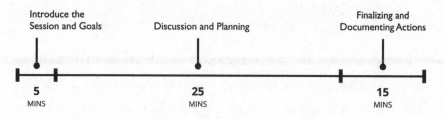

Fig. 9.2: Summit Session Structure

The number one goal to emphasize is that we want to get to tangible next steps. The goal of the event is to have clarity on not just what work is going to happen, but who is doing it and when it should be done by. The final fifteen minutes are designed to capture these actions.

Not all sessions will accomplish this, and we shouldn't be too hard on community members if they don't. We should, though, set these next steps as a standard goal for sessions.

Ideally, these actions should be captured on a public website (such as a wiki) so those not at the event can follow along. When the event is completed, you can then take these actions and provide any additional support to community members as they work on them (or even incorporate them in your Quarterly Delivery Plan).

Step 3. Run the Event

The major risk of any sprint is a lot of ideation and talk and no concrete action. As you facilitate your event, encourage people to make the most out of the time together. Have key decisions and debates, explore new ideas, but really focus everyone on action. *You want people to leave the sprint with a sense of accomplishment and substance.*

If possible, *try to allow people who cannot join the event to dial in.* This opens the event up to your broader community and makes it more inclusive. Where possible, provide three key services (in order of priority):

1. *Provide a live stream so that people can listen in* from outside the event. This may be a conference call or a video stream. Ensure these streams are linked from the schedule so people can join easily.

2. *Provide a real-time chat channel* that all attendees inside and outside the conference can join. For each discussion session room, create a different chat channel people can join to interact with the session as they listen to it.

3. *Have a projector that displays the chat channel for that session room.* This provides a way for attendees to see if someone from outside the conference has a contribution to the discussion.

This blend of in-person and remote participation provides a great way to harness face-to-face communication and makes it accessible to everyone, including those online.

As the event wraps, have a closing party where attendees can celebrate all the work invested together, have fun, and blow off some steam. One approach we used at every Ubuntu Developer Summit was to put together a live band, where any attendee was welcome to join and play songs together.[7] It helped solidify lasting friendships and camaraderie. Also, who doesn't want to play "Freebird" with their friends?

Step 4. Follow Through after the Event

Here's the critical point: everyone invested a lot of time in the event, so *make it stick*. Review all the plans made and ensure that you follow up with people who committed to work to deliver on it.

Follow through on the decisions made, provide updates on progress, and break down problems and blockers.

These events are only useful if the community makes plans they can deliver on. Not everything will get done, but the majority of the agreed work should be executed. This is not just important to ensure the event was worth everyone's time but also to ensure that the event itself adds value to the community.

A FOCUS ON FUSION

Some of the best things in life are the result of *fusion*: French and Thai food, jazz and metal music, Shakespearian tales with a Quentin Tarantino twist—they are all interesting. Sometimes fusion works and sometimes it doesn't; it requires experimentation.

The in-person and digital realms benefit from fusion, but this requires similar experimentation. Try new ideas. How can you better hook your events into your digital community? How can your broader community play a role in live events? How can you refine how your sessions are run? How can you better support your session leaders and keynotes?

Fortunately, technology makes this easier and easier as time passes, but it depends on you as a leader to drive this experimentation.

CHAPTER 10

Integrate, Evolve, and Build

Growth is never by mere chance; it is the result of forces working together.

—James Cash (J. C.) Penney

L ife doesn't exist in a vacuum. You can train hard and never kick a ball, run a race, or compete in a competition. You can plan to lose weight and never get on the treadmill. In other words, *plans don't mean squat if we can't put them into action.*

Throughout this book we have built a robust foundation and strategy for our community. We have approached it from the right perspective, to build value for you and your members, and we have designed it so that every piece of detail maps to our broader strategic goals. But here's the deal: *you need to integrate it into your organization, hire the right people to deliver it, and most importantly, build organizational capabilities.*

Building organizational muscle is about becoming self-sufficient. Our strategic development gets us a plan to execute, but what builds organizational capabilities is how you integrate that strategy into your organization, execute, and then learn from the experience. This chapter covers how to do this. Let's begin by exploring how we hire the right people, and then we will cover integrating our strategy into the organization.

HIRING COMMUNITY MANAGEMENT STAFF

Hiring solid community management staff is essential to the overall success of your initiative. Unfortunately, this can introduce wrinkles into our plan. As a general rule, I have found most people who work professionally in a community fall into one of three buckets:

1. *Community Director.* These are the most senior people who work in the industry. They should be able to operate at the level we are discussing in this book and be able to understand business requirements, produce a value proposition for the community, and build a strategy that delivers it. They should be sophisticated communicators and have experience working with other teams and stakeholders to deliver their strategy. They should also be able to engage with the community directly, build relationships, and be excellent communicators in both written and spoken form.

Sadly these people are few and far between. The majority are already working in well-compensated positions and will only switch companies if (a) the opportunity is interesting, (b) they are well compensated, and (c) they would have influence in your organization. They are a godsend when you can find them.

2. *Community Manager.* These people will be less experienced and senior, but they should be good solid workhorses. They are usually less strategic and more tactical in nature but should have good project management skills. They should be execution focused, cranking through work, responding to members, and balancing many relationships concurrently in your community. Some are very technical in nature, often previously working as engineers. Members of your community will build strong relationships with community managers, who have more bandwidth to dedicate to them.

3. *Community Evangelist.* These folks are usually focused on delivering information and knowledge to your community and beyond. They are typically engaging and dynamic personalities, and natural show people. They should be excellent writers and speakers, and typically travel extensively getting out to speak to, meet, and build relationships with your community.

Many evangelists are less strategic in nature, as their work is focused specifically on outreach and awareness. As such, be careful: I have known companies to hire an evangelist presuming they had the strategic chops, only to find that their expertise and value was quite different.

To be clear, there are many who blend these different levels of expertise together, so don't take this delineation too literally. There are also variations on these roles such as Developer Relations, Community Specialist, and Community Associate, but those are mostly different mixtures of the above three buckets (some with specialization included).

As a general rule, if you are starting a new community, you should focus on getting a solid Community Director or Community

Manager first. You may need to supplement them with strategic support and mentoring depending on their experience (this is the work I often do with clients). Hire an evangelist when you feel comfortable strategically and are focusing on building growth and engagement.

What to Look For

Let me be clear about something: *hiring community leadership staff is a pain in the butt.* Unlike other professions (such as software engineers), which have a strong focus on a single discipline (e.g., engineering), community leadership staff need to be able to straddle multiple disciplines such as workflow, engagement, and technology.

Whether you are looking for a Community Director, Community Manager, or Community Evangelist, here are three dimensions to judge them on:

- *Domain Expertise.* Does this person have expertise in your specific domain, be it your products/services, market, or something else? If you need someone to work with a technical community, do they understand the technology? More importantly, do they understand the needs of the people who build that technology?
- *People Person.* Is this person motivated and excited to work with people? Do they thrive on building relationships, engaging with contributors, and providing surprise and delight at a human, interpersonal level? It is very difficult to train someone to be a people person, so they need to have an instinctive interest in it. Just

because someone is affable in an interview doesn't mean they are intrinsically a *people* person. Get to the heart of what motivates them about their work: Are human experiences at the center of it?

- *Willingness to Grow.* Finally, are they humble in their expertise, comfortable in failing forward, and willing to grow? Community strategy and leadership is a rapidly changing art and science that is heavily dependent on the specific context and operations of that individual community and organization. *Great leaders don't have all the answers, no matter what level they ascend to.* You need someone who can think creatively, be able to always push forward to refine and improve, and never assume they have all the answers. Humility and a willingness to grow are key requirements.

This is where it gets tricky. Few people have all of these ingredients. Prioritize finding a people person who has a willingness to grow. These are intrinsic human instincts that are difficult to teach. I once hired someone who primarily had great domain expertise but just couldn't engage effectively with people. Sadly, I had to let him go.

If you do hire someone who lacks domain expertise, assess how quickly they can learn it and if they have an interest in it. You need someone with passion for the focus of your community (e.g., your product, service, or focus); this will provide the drive to help them pick it up quickly. It is difficult to train someone who doesn't give a crap about the topic of the community.

If you are looking to hire a Community Director, there is one more element to stir into the mixing bowl. Find a *strategically minded "doer."* They need to be able to build a strategy that maps well with the company's desired value, broader business and community objectives, and other teams and stakeholders. You need someone who can work across departments, who is collaborative, and who has the bit between their teeth to deliver. They need to be calm in the face of pushback. They are going to face many roadblocks, and you need someone who can navigate them.

Where to Find Them

First put together a job description and run it past other leaders you know who have hired a similar role in other communities. Make sure you emphasize the responsibilities so you can attract the right kind of people. Unfortunately, I don't have space here to share role descriptions, but you can find templates by heading to https://www.jonobacon.com and selecting Resources.

Promote the role and source candidates as best you can, but *be careful with recruiters*. They are historically terrible at understanding the nuances of these kinds of roles and pull in lots of unqualified candidates (and annoy the qualified ones). *Tap your network, reach out to those connected to good candidates, and seek referrals.*

There are two primary ways to find people, one of which costs more but gets results faster. The other way is cheaper but can build lasting commitment.

1. *Hire Away.* The best candidates already have well-compensated roles in companies they likely enjoy working for. If you want to increase the likelihood of bringing in A-grade talent, try to hire someone out of their existing role. *This requires exceeding their*

compensation package and providing an exciting opportunity where they can continue to grow their career. Most don't just want more money for more of the same; they want career growth and more meaningful work.

The benefit of this approach is that you can bring in a solid foundation more quickly.

2. *Mentor In.* The longer, but cheaper approach is to run the standard recruitment process and try finding someone who has the best combination of ingredients we discussed earlier. This can result in some less qualified candidates who are blisteringly enthusiastic, don't require as high a salary, and are excited about the opportunity to learn and grow. Another option here is to recruit someone who already works for you so they switch jobs to this role.

The critical component of this approach is to *have a clear mentoring program in place.* When this person joins (or switches roles if they already work for you), you should have clarity on which of the ingredients I outlined earlier (domain expertise, people person, willingness to grow, strategically minded doer) needs the most focus and work.

Ensure that they have a clear set of goals to accomplish in their first six months (this is where the Quarterly Delivery Plan comes in), and provide someone who can mentor and support them through their growth. For example, I commonly provide mentoring to clients.

When you deliver this mentoring well, it can grow a remarkable level of commitment. The new hire will feel that the company invested in them and will often stay committed and focused for many years.

Where They Should Report In

This is a tricky one. I have worked with community managers who have reported into marketing, some who report into engineering, some who report to the CEO/CTO, and some who even report into product.

CEO/Founders. If community is going to be a critical component of your organization with key investment, ideally, they will be a top-level department with their own budget, can join executive team meetings, and their performance will be judged by the CEO or a founder. This is only recommended for Community Directors who have primary strategic focus and recommended for small companies and start-ups.

Marketing. If your community is a Consumer or Champion type, reporting into marketing may be a natural fit. Carefully assess how well your marketing team understands the value of communities and is willing to support this work.

Unfortunately, some marketing leaders are either deeply suspicious that community could be a threat to them, or don't understand the dynamics. Don't inadvertently make them a blocker for your hires. To reduce this risk, test your marketing lead. Get them to read this book and see how well they pick up the subject matter!

Engineering. If your community is a Collaborator type or technical in nature, reporting into engineering may make more sense. Many of my clients have staff who report into the CEO/Founder initially and later move to report into the CTO (who may run engineering). It makes a lot of sense for community staff to be in meetings with engineering leads to (a) understand their workflow and needs better (which will impact community members), and (b) build closer relationships with them and their teams.

Product. In some companies, particularly technology firms, the product team is the bridge between customers/users and the product. As such, this can be a logical fit *if* there is a clear understanding of the audience and the value of a community in supporting it.

Wherever the role(s) report in, you will need to ensure your departments are aligned. This is where the strategy we have built plays a key role in ensuring everyone is on the same page with delivery and how they will collaborate.

BAKING YOUR STRATEGY INTO YOUR BUSINESS

"Ultimately, community participation is in our DNA. We recognize that open source is an ecosystem, so we understand the importance of giving back." This is what Jim Whitehurst, CEO of Red Hat, said to me when I asked him about lessons learned balancing the needs of a company and community.[1]

> Red Hat contributes to dozens of open-source communities in areas where we don't have commercial products. We do this because these are areas important to the open-source communities in which we are active, and the work needs to be done. We understand that there is value in contributing whether or not there is a direct quid pro quo. It's part of what's made us successful.

Jim has a clear vision of where community fits in his organization, the expectations of his team, and where the line is drawn between the company and community. This isn't always clear, particularly in companies who are new to building communities. As such, there are five key ways of bringing this clarity and reducing the risk of your strategy falling apart.

1. Community Is Everyone's Priority

Mårten Mickos summarized it best when he enthusiastically stated that, "Everyone needs to know a hacker." He saw the importance of everyone, not just community leadership staff, having a relationship with, understanding the needs of, and engaging with their community. *Good leadership trickles down, and if your leadership demonstrates good community habits, your staff will too.*

Ideally your leadership team should be regularly participating in your community platforms, even if only two or three times a week. They should ask and expect their teams to participate too. Provide training to help them get started and make it a daily habit. Celebrate and reward cases where your staff demonstrates quality community engagement; this will encourage others to follow suit.

It may sound aggressive, but your departmental leads should ideally have their performance review incorporate some form of community engagement. Clear performance requirements (and accountability) should be well understood. You assess their performance on product and business dimensions, so why not community dimensions too?

Similarly, you need to inject the focus and importance of the community everywhere you can. Your company values should embody it. Your strategic planning should embody it. Your marketing should embody it. My most successful clients regularly ask "How can this add value to our community?" in product meetings.

This all takes work, but an integral cultural understanding of the community's importance in your organization will significantly increase your chances of success.

2. Get Departmental Alignment

People often presume they are aligned and solving the same problems when they actually have subtly different interpretations. It took me a long time to realize this.

Departments are usually on board in the early ideation phase of a community strategy, but things often break down when they need to execute. This is why we created our Big Rocks earlier and our more detailed Quarterly Delivery Plan. These two documents crisply define *what* we are going to do, *which* results we want to see, and *who* ultimately has responsibility for delivery.

Ensure that all departments are clearly aligned in what role they play in delivering community strategy. Make this an explicit discussion. Can each department commit the time and resources to deliver their responsibilities for each of the Big Rocks? If not, either expand your resources or be more conservative in your objectives. Either way, there needs to be (a) commitment to delivery, and (b) an understanding that *not delivering is not an option*.

The companies I see that fail at community strategy (and other areas too) operate in a culture in which not delivering agreed-upon goals is OK. Let's fix that now: *not delivering is not OK*. Reevaluating goals, paring down work, and otherwise adjusting based on the realities of running a business and community is fine, but rolling out excuse after excuse for not hitting the target is not.

3. Operate on a Cadence Cycle

Back in chapter 6, I presented my Cadence-Based Community Cycle:

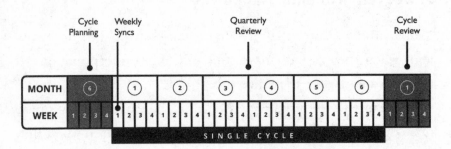

As we discussed back then, there is enormous value to building a strategic cycle that repeats; it bakes in organizational skills and optimization. It also presents a chance to pull different people and stakeholders in at the right time to ensure your strategy is on the right track. I have seen these cycles work with multiple clients and in communities such as Pop!_OS, Fedora, and Ubuntu.

It works like this:

Item	Who Should Be There?	Focus
Cycle Planning	Key stakeholders, departmental leads, key community members	Finalize key areas of work, get input from community members, get approval from stakeholders, and ensure departmental ownership and delivery is clear. This sets the stage for the next two quarters.

Weekly Syncs	Owners of items in the quarterly plan, execution staff, and required community members	Weekly review of the Quarterly Delivery Plan with a focus on unblocking problems, clarifying points of collaboration between departments/community teams, and resolving any other issues.
Quarterly Review	Departmental leads	After each quarter, all departmental leads should review overall delivery so far and identify any issues and blockers and how to resolve them. Small adjustments to KPIs may be made based on work in-flight.
Cycle Review	Key stakeholders, departmental leads, and relevant staff and community members	At the end of the cycle, bring together key stakeholders, departmental leads, and others to review (a) the value of the work delivered, (b) how well the team delivered it, and (c) areas of optimization and improvement that can be put in place for the next cycle.

Integrate this cadence into your schedules and planning. *Get these meetings scheduled now* (so people don't book over them with trips and vacations).

Remember, we are building organizational muscle here. Just like building muscle on your body, routine is what makes us tick. Regular workouts, predictable mealtimes, consistent bedtimes . . . they all build rigor and predictability that results in consistent habits and tangible results. Do the same with this cadence cycle. Every time you run the cycle, you will learn how to optimize and make it more efficient every time.

4. Train and Mentor

One major lesson I have learned from consulting with so many companies is that communities are just weird for many people, and they often struggle in getting started and participating. Their employees are often initially reluctant to participate, fearful of making missteps (particularly with a public community), and sometimes confused about what exactly they should be doing. The solution here is *education* and *mentoring*.

Make it clear why this work is important. Don't just tell them to do the work. Help them to understand the *value* of it. In meetings, company-wide memos and posts, and all-hands sessions, always focus on how the community enriches your organization, the work you do, and future potential. How does it make their job more interesting, fulfilling, and valuable? Sell them on it and get them excited about playing a role in it.

This vision and inspiration need to be backed up with a practical way they can engage. Make it clear what you expect from them. Get specific. What exactly do you want your team to do?

On one hand this should be simple: you can point them to your Quarterly Delivery Plan. On the other hand, how do you want them to participate in the community? Which tools should they use? Which problems should they solve? How long should they spend each day (I recommend a minimum of fifteen minutes a day)? How do you want them to engage with your community members (e.g., providing encouragement, solving problems, etc.)? Be clear in what you expect and give them *very specific goals to accomplish.*

For example, one tool I often use to build communities, Discourse, has a "trust model" through which I can easily track if people are participating effectively.[2] A member's trust level increases the more they proactively participate, not just in reading content but also writing, filling out their profile, having their content liked, and more. Give your employees goals (e.g., achieving a specific trust level) and set expectations on daily participation and time required so they can build a habit.

Be honest with people: they are going to screw up. Make it clear how failures can be handled (e.g., removing accidental disclosures or confidential content), and that the organization expects mistakes to be made. Make it clear that there will be no dragging over the coals while people learn how to do this.

Always have a way in which staff can reach out and get help. Provide documentation they can read to answer common questions. Most people naturally don't ask for help, so schedule regular check-ins to see how they are doing and regularly tap them on the shoulder privately to see how they are doing personally and if you can help.

It is recommended you put in place at least three to six training sessions to cover these areas, including clear goals and next steps for employees to follow. Set daily expectations of participating in the community, even if that participation is just fifteen minutes a day. Ask them to schedule it in their calendars. Remember, it takes sixty-six days to build a habit, and we need them to build the habit of participating in the community every day.

Also put in place clear mentoring programs (typically with your Community Director/Manager) to provide guidance after the training completes. You need the right balance of setting expectations that lack of participation is not an option but also that they have ample support and guidance to get involved and be successful.

5. Execute, Review, Repeat

Start delivering work and have the meetings outlined earlier in the cadence cycle. Watch how well things go. *Don't just judge if your team delivers. Judge how they deliver and any problems they face.* Look for dents in your armor and holes in the road so you can better support your team and avoid further issues.

In each Quarterly Review and Cycle Review discuss these dents and bumps openly with your team. *Have an unemotional conversation about how to rectify them in the future.* What was successfully delivered? What wasn't, and why? Were there process or team issues we should smooth out? How can the leadership team better support staff? See every problem as an opportunity for future improvement, get agreement on how you will implement those changes, and then review again at the next Quarterly Review or Cycle Review.

Importantly, don't just focus on the flaws. *Celebrate the successes.* Celebrate the work that is delivered, the skills that are developed, and the successes your team and your community enjoy.

PERFECTION IS NOT REQUIRED, BUT FOCUS IS

If any of you reading this have run a business before, you know that not everything goes according to plan. Decisions have to be made quicker than expected, we have fewer resources than we would like, problems hunt together in packs, and opportunity can sometimes be tricky to find in our more challenging moments.

The problem with a lot of business books is that they often provide recommendations for how to do something that adds value, all while rather conveniently ignoring the reality of the world around us. I want to kick that habit.

You don't have to have a perfect strategy. You don't have to have it perfectly integrated into your business. You do, though, need a few key skills: *to put together a plan, execute it, and improve it with experience.* Learn by doing, and do by learning. Treat every problem as a teachable moment and every success as a validation of your approach. Look at your work unemotionally as a set of logical connections in which you are always finding ways to optimize the logic. This is how we truly bake these skills into your organization.

CHAPTER 11

Onward and Upward

Good company in a journey makes the way seem shorter.

—Izaak Walton

You made it. We have covered a lot of ground and are now getting into the closing lap.

Writing this book was a rather complicated endeavor. The value, opportunity, and approach to building productive communities is a topic that could span ten books. Heck, it could span one hundred books.

Cherry-picking the most important elements of this journey and assembling them into a pragmatic methodology that can map to many different types of organization—well, let me just say it wasn't exactly a walk in the park. I hope you have felt it was not only worth the price on the back of the book but also worth the time invested in reading it.

If there is something I hope you have picked up throughout these pages, it is that I am a no-BS kind of guy. Here is another piece of no BS: *you are only just getting started, and to get good at this you need to immerse yourself in an always-evolving stream of content, methods, and expertise.*

The sum total of expertise on this topic is not just contained in these pages. I have taken a throaty whack at assembling what I felt were a key set of ideas and approaches for a primer, but it is essential that you *keep on keeping on.* We are only as good as the ideas, approaches, and experiences that we are exposed to.

So, as we near the end of our time together in these pages, I want to share some recommendations for not just how to maintain your forward momentum, but also how we can continue to build our relationship too.

WAYS TO KEEP LEARNING

There are five key things you should do to continue learning, growing, and setting you and your team up for the most success in understanding how to build communities:

1. *Read this book again. Seriously.* It might seem trite, but I mean it. As you read this book the first time, you were taking in a lot of information, the vast majority of which is likely new to you. You may have read it while lying in bed before you nodded off, or on a beach or a busy commuter train. Our brains get distracted and we miss things.

There is a lot of detail in these pages, and rereading will not just help with what did soak in, but it will be a valuable "second scan" for the bits you missed. It will also give you the benefit of reading the earlier parts of the book while knowing more about where we are ultimately getting to. This really does help to seal those principles in your brain.

2. *Surround yourself with new ideas.* Earlier in my career I made the mistake of thinking I had much of this figured out. Then I quit my job, went and worked somewhere else, and realized there was so, so much I had yet to learn.

Read other books and articles. Find people who have read this book and discuss and debate it with them. Put yourself in a position to expand your understanding of the material I have presented and augment it with new ideas and approaches. Take my methods, hack them, and improve them. This will all help to provide a full complement of material to help you shape your own approach.

3. *Interview and ask questions.* There are thousands of people out there who have been a part of both successful and unsuccessful communities. If you are new at this, one of the best things you can do is learn from the old (and young!) hands.

Reach out to them, hop on a call, ask them questions, and understand their experiences. Community people love to talk—they will take the call. Tease out the elements of their approach that you can harness in your own work. You are sure to have a number of "aha!" moments in these discussions as elements of the journey become clearer.

4. *Test and challenge your assumptions.* As you have read through this book, you will have made a series of assumptions. Some of them will be accurate, and some of them won't. This is perfectly normal.

Convert your assumptions into *hypotheses.* Test and learn from them. Do you presume social media is a waste of time? Do you think people won't want to create content for your community? Do you think travel is a waste of money? Do you think you can't possibly make an annual Big Rocks plan? Treat everything as a test condition, and it will keep your mind open and your feet on the ground.

5. *Document, share, and discuss.* Throughout this book I have drummed in the importance of openness and transparency in communities. In keeping with this theme, one of the best things you can do is to share your experiences building your community. This can be on a blog, podcast, video, or somewhere else.

Talk about your work, gather further feedback, and continue to evolve. Don't forget to keep me posted on how you are doing at jono@jonobacon.com. I always *love* to hear about how my readers are doing!

Be vulnerable. Share what worked and what didn't. None of us are perfect, myself included. Being vulnerable not only generates respect from the people you work with, but it also invites an opportunity to discuss new approaches and ideas. Encourage your audience to provide their feedback and comments.

KEEP ON KEEPING ON

I will always remember when I first discovered the potential of communities. It was 1998 and my brother Simon had just introduced me to a rather nerdy, quite-unknown-at-the-time computer operating system called Linux. At the time I worked part-time at a bookstore, so I used my staff discount to buy a book about it.

In that book I discovered that Linux, and the broader open-source ecosystem, was built by a global community of mostly volunteers. Sure, the tech was interesting, but it was this global-community-working-together bit that really switched a lightbulb on in my mind.

I decided back then, in my barely pubescent teenage peanut of a brain, that I was going to make it my life's mission to understand every nuance of how all of this works, and to help other people to see and harness the value of these communities too.

As such, this book is just one component in this mission. I have a raft of additional resources available, and I recommend you head to https://www.jonobacon.com and follow three steps to plug yourself in:

Step 1. Use the Resources. Select Resources in the menu to see a raft of resources that support the content in this book. This includes sample personas, on-ramps, job descriptions, incentives, content ideas, and more.

Step 2. Read the Blog. Click or tap on Blog and be sure to see my articles. Every month I write new content with pragmatic recommendations covering community strategy, incentives, metrics, behavioral economics, tools and platforms, social media, leadership, and more. This book is a firm foundation, and this monthly content will continue to expand and grow your experience and capabilities.

Step 3. Join as a Member. Finally, click or tap on Join and consider signing up as a member. This is entirely free and comes with a raft of benefits such as new material delivered directly to you; exclusive member-only content, events, and opportunities; one-on-one workshops with me; early access to new books and projects; and more.

Importantly, I take care of my members, and I will never spam you or sell your details (people who do this are the barnacles of humanity). This is the best way to always stay up to date and keep developing your skills and experience.

You may also want to follow me on social media:

- Twitter—https://www.twitter.com/jonobacon
- Facebook—https://www.facebook.com/jonobacon
- LinkedIn—https://www.linkedin.com/in/jonobacon
- YouTube—https://www.youtube.com/jonobacon
- Instagram—https://www.instagram.com/jonobacongram/

If you follow me on any of these, be sure to say hi!

Finally, I love to hear from my readers. Drop me a line at jono@jonobacon.com and let me know what you are doing and what you thought of this book.

WORKING TOGETHER

When I started writing this book, one of the main goals that I set out with was to not make it seem like a giant bulging advert for my consulting services. I have read too many business books that do this. Books should be for sharing ideas, experience, and insight, not for shoving commercial ambitions down someone's throat. I am already embarrassed enough to call myself a consultant (due to so many snake-oil consultants out there). The last thing I wanted to do was to add this book to that turgid pile of pitches masquerading as books.

Being mindful of this though, it would be remiss if I didn't share a little about how I work with organizations to help them build communities, as some of you might actually find this helpful. So, let me keep this simple, concise, and importantly, reserved to these last few pages of the book. You can safely skip this if you are uninterested.

In a nutshell, I work with clients to help them build communities either wrapped around a public product, service, or platform, or communities within the walls of their organization (often designed to break down silos and improve how their teams work together).

I usually work with my clients to help them build out their community strategy, and mentor and train their team in the execution and delivery of it. I also provide speaking (both corporate and conferences), training, and support. My approach is to not just help an organization put together a strategy but to integrate the skills to do it themselves into their team and make me ultimately irrelevant.

You can find out more about my consulting services by heading to https://www.jonobacon.com/consulting. If you would like to talk more about working together, drop me an email at jono@jonobacon.com.

PEACE OUT

As I write this, at thirty thousand feet on my way from San Francisco to Edinburgh for a business trip, it has been twenty years since I was first exposed to communities. It has subsequently been a twenty-year journey trying to soak up as much as I can about *why* and *how* we build powerful, thriving communities. I have worked hard to really understand and sieve the signal from the noise. As with everything, this is a constant journey, but one that is a blast to be on.

Throughout these twenty years I, and many of you, have seen the darker elements of humanity. Despotic regimes, unnecessary conflicts and wars, an increasingly narcissistic online culture, political tensions, etc. It is tempting to turn on the news and question our collective faith in the human condition and whether the potential I have shared in these pages is all just an optimistic pipe dream.

But then I think of Abayomi, our young friend in Africa who I talked about right at the beginning of this book. I think about the rich tapestry of technology, content, experiences, and ideas that have been generated around the world by people working together. I think about the legion of unsung heroes who get up every day to create, mentor, support, and cheerlead the success of others. I think of the thousands of careers that have been forged, the businesses started, and the dreams turned into reality—all because we are more powerful together than as individuals. I see a flip-book in my head of the thousands of people I have met over the years that have grown into the measure of the person they wanted to be because they were bolstered by the community condition.

People are remarkable. We all have an amazing capacity for kindness, counsel, and courage, and when we are surrounded by those with similar traits, we become better. *The human condition is not a fearful, angry, divided one. It is a social and supportive one. We thrive together.*

This book is dedicated to that condition. When we can dream big and put in place a set of guardrails to make that dream happen, the world is our oyster. That has been my hope for this book. I can't wait to see what you all come up with!

Best of luck. Let me know how you get on, and let me know if there is anything I can ever help with. I want you all to succeed and thrive, no matter what you are working on. Rock on!

Notes

ACKNOWLEDGMENTS

1. "Become a Member," Jono Bacon, accessed January 9, 2019, https://www.jonobacon.com/join/.

FOREWORD

1. Charles Lindbergh, *Spirit of St. Louis* (New York: Charles Scribner's Sons, 1953), 25, 34, 77, 102.

2. Michelle Evans, "5 Stats You Need to Know About Connected Consumers," *Forbes*, August 22, 2017, https://www.forbes.com /sites/michelleevans1/2017/08/22/5-stats-you-need-to-know-about -connected-consumers-in-2017/#7909aeec1962; Peter Diamandis, "4 Billion New Minds Online: The Coming Era of Connectivity," *Singularity*, July 27, 2018, https://singularityhub.com/2018/07/27 /4-billion-new-minds-online-the-coming-era-of-connectivity/#sm .000qnxowz119ye48z0yl04iujpn9p.

3. Tibi Puiu, "Your Smartphone Is Millions of Times More Powerful Than All of NASA's Combined Computing in 1969," *ZMEScience*, February 15, 2019, https://www.zmescience.com/research /technology/smartphone-power-compared-to-apollo-432/.

1: WHAT IS A COMMUNITY AND WHY DO YOU NEED TO BUILD ONE?

1. "What Was It Like to Be Online During the 80s?" *Gizmodo*, September 25, 2014, https://gizmodo.com/what-it-was-like-to-be -on-the-internet-during-the-80s-1638800803; Benj Edwards, "The

Lost Civilization of Dial-Up Bulletin Board Systems," *The Atlantic*, November 4, 2016, https://www.theatlantic.com/technology /archive/2016/11/the-lost-civilization-of-dial-up-bulletin-board -systems/506465/.

2. "Textfilesdotcom," Text Files, accessed March 1, 2019, http://www .textfiles.com/.

3. "About the GNU Project," GNU, accessed March 1, 2019, https://www.gnu.org/gnu/thegnuproject.en.html.

4. Calvin Reid, "Random House Acquires Figment," *Publisher's Weekly*, October 29, 2013, https://www.publishersweekly.com/pw/by-topic /childrens/childrens-industry-news/article/59745-random-house -acquires-figment.html.

5. "Lego Ideas: Community," LEGO.com, accessed November 2, 2018, https://ideas.lego.com/community?query=&sort=most_submissions.

6. Asher Madan, "Xbox Live Grows to 59 Million Active Users," Windows Central, January 31, 2018, https://www.windowscentral.com /xbox-live-grew-59-million-active-users-last-quarter.

7. "SAP Community Home," SAP, accessed November 2, 2018, https://www.sap.com/community.html.

8. Jagdish N. Sheth and Rajendra S. Sisodia, *Does Marketing Need Reform?: Fresh Perspectives on the Future* (London: Routledge, 2006), 111.

9. Rose Eveleth, "How Much Is Wikipedia Worth?," *Smithsonian*, October 7, 2013, https://www.smithsonianmag.com/smart-news/how-much-is -wikipedia-worth-704865/.

10. "Community and Collaboration," Open Source Initiative, accessed March 2, 2019, https://opensource.org/community.

11. Javelin VP, "The Power of Collaborative Media," *Medium*, January 31, 2019, https://medium.com/@JavelinVP/power-of-collaborative-media -d6c32e617f71.

12. Juliana J. Bolden, "Video: Joseph Gordon-Levitt on 'HitRecord on TV' on Winning an Emmy Award," *Television Academy*, August 14, 2014, http://www.emmys.com/news/industry-news/video-joseph -gordon-levitt-hitrecord-tv-winning-an-emmy-award.

13. Joseph Gordon-Levitt, telephone interview with Jono Bacon, November 7, 2018.

14. Kate Clark, "Joseph Gordon-Levitt's Artist Collaboration Platform HitRecord Raises $6.4m," *TechCrunch*, January 31, 2019,

https://techcrunch.com/2019/01/31/joseph-gordon-levitts-artist
-collaboration-platform-hitrecord-raises-6-4m/.

15. "Star Citizen by Cloud Imperium Games Corporation," Kickstarter, accessed November 1, 2018, https://www.kickstarter.com/projects /cig/star-citizen; P. Ariyasinghe, "Star Citizen Hits $150 Million in Crowd Funding," Neowin, May 20, 2017, https://www.neowin.net /news/star-citizen-hits-150-million-in-crowd-funding/.

16. Lizette Chapman and Eric Newcomer, "Software Maker Docker Is Raising Funding at $1.3 Billion Valuation," *Bloomberg*, August 9, 2017, https://www.bloomberg.com/news/articles/2017-08-09/docker -is-said-to-be-raising-funding-at-1-3-billion-valuation.

17. Johana Bhuiyan, "Drivers Don't Trust Uber. This Is How It's Trying to Win Them Back," Recode, February 5, 2018, https://www.recode. net/2018/2/5/16777536/uber-travis-kalanick-recruit-drivers-tipping; Chris Matyszczyk "United Airlines Was Just Ranked Lower Than America's Most Controversial Airline in Customer Satisfaction," *Inc.*, May 30, 2018, https://www.inc.com/chris-matyszczyk/united-airlines -was-just-ranked-lower-than-americas-most-controversial-airline-in -customer-satisfaction.html; Tom Chandler, "The Death of MySpace," Young Academic, March 31, 2011, https://www.youngacademic.co.uk /features/the-death-of-myspace-young-academic-columns-953; Charles Arthur, "Digg Loses a Third of Its Visitors in a Month: Is It Dead?," *The Guardian*, June 3, 2010, https://www.theguardian.com /technology/blog/2010/jun/03/digg-dead-falling-visitors.

18. Emily Richardson, "Globally Offensive: Let's Talk About Abuse in CS:GO," *Rock Paper Shotgun*, July 17, 2015, https://www.rockpapershotgun.com/2015/07/17/cs-go-abuse/.

19. "Support," Fractal Audio Systems, accessed March 2, 2019, https://www.fractalaudio.com/support/.

20. "Axe Change—The Official Site for Fractal Audio Presets, Cabs and More," Axe Change, accessed March 2, 2019, http://axechange .fractalaudio.com/.

21. Dan Ariely, "What Makes Us Feel Good About Our Work?," TED, October 2012, https://www.ted.com/talks/dan_ariely_what_makes _us_feel_good_about_our_work.

22. "Salesforce Customers List," Sales Inside, accessed May 2, 2018, https:// www.salesinsideinc.com/services-details/salesforce-customers-list.

23. "Salesforce Trailblazer Community," Salesforce, accessed February 25, 2019, https://success.salesforce.com/.

24. "Firefox Crop Circle,"FirefoxCropCircle.com, accessed November 30, 2018, https://firefoxcropcircle.com/circle/; "SpreadFirefox," Mozilla Firefox, November 2013, https://blog.mozilla.org/press/files/2013 /11/nytimes-firefox-final.pdf.

25. "Pebble Time—Awesome Smartwatch, No Compromises," Kickstarter, accessed November 25, 2018, https://www.kickstarter.com/projects /getpebble/pebble-time-awesome-smartwatch-no-compromises /description; "Exploding Kittens," Kickstarter, accessed November 25, 2018, https://www.kickstarter.com/projects/elanlee/exploding -kittens/description.

26. Haydn Taylor, "Minecraft Exceeds 90m Monthly Active Users," Games Industry, October 2, 2018, https://www.gamesindustry.biz/articles /2018-10-02-minecraft-exceeds-90-million-monthly-active-users.

27. Minecraft Forum, accessed January 9, 2019, https://www.mine craftforum.net/forums; Minecraft Wiki, accessed January 9, 2019, https://minecraft.gamepedia.com/Minecraft_Wiki.

28. Alex Sherman, and Lora Kolodny, "IBM to Acquire Red Hat in Deal Valued at $34 Billion," CNBC, October 28, 2018, https://www.cnbc.com/2018/10/28/ibm-to-acquire-red-hat-in-deal -valued-at-34-billion.html.

29. Jim Whitehurst, email interview with Jono Bacon, November 26, 2018.

30. Desire Athow, "Linux Costs USD 10.8 billion to Build Says Linux Foundation," IT Pro Portal, October 23, 2018, https://www.itprop ortal.com/2008/10/23/linux-costs-usd-108-billion-build-says-linux -foundation/.

31. Paul Sawers, "WordPress Now Powers 30% of Websites, VentureBeat, March 5, 2018, https://venturebeat.com/2018/03/05/wordpress-now -powers-30-of-websites/.

32. Liz Lanier, "'Star Citizen' Reaches $200 Million in Funding From 171 Countries," *Variety*, November 19, 2018, https://variety.com/2018 /gaming/news/star-citizen-reaches-200-million-1203032223/.

2: CONSUMERS, CHAMPIONS, AND COLLABORATORS

1. "The History Of Iron Maiden—Part One," 1:30:33, YouTube video, October 13, 2017, https://youtu.be/qDc5Px5f0OE?t=4308.

2. Tom Hanks, *A League of Their Own*, directed by Penny Marshall (Culver City, CA: Columbia Pictures, 1992).

3. xprize.org. (2019). Mojave Aerospace Ventures Wins The Competition That Started It All. [online] Available at: https://www.xprize.org/prizes/ansari/articles/mojave-aerospace-ventures-wins-the-competition [Accessed 29 Mar. 2019].

4. "The Trek BBS," TrekBBS, accessed May 17, 2018, https://www.trekbbs.com/.

5. "Ardour—The Digital Audio Workstation," Ardour, accessed May 25, 2018, https://ardour.org/.

6. "/r/science metrics (Science)," Reddit Metrics, accessed May 9, 2018, http://redditmetrics.com/r/science. "/r/Sneakers metrics (Sneakerheads Unite!)," Reddit Metrics, accessed May 9, 2018, http://redditmetrics.com/r/Sneakers.

7. Internet Archive, "The Long Tail," *Wired Blogs*, September 8, 2005, https://web.archive.org/web/20170310130052/http://www.longtail.com/the_long_tail/2005/09/long_tail_101.html.

8. "PSY–Gangnam Style," 4:12, YouTube video, July 15, 2012, https://www.youtube.com/watch?v=9bZkp7q19f0.

9. "Study Finds Our Desire for 'Like-Minded Others' Is Hard-Wired," University of Kansas, February 23, 2016, https://news.ku.edu/2016/02/19/new-study-finds-our-desire-minded-others-hard-wired-controls-friend-and-partner.

10. "Market Brief—2018 Digital Games & Interactive Entertainment Industry Year in Review," SuperData Research, accessed May 25, 2018, https://www.superdataresearch.com/market-data/market-brief-year-in-review/.

11. IGN Boards, accessed May 25, 2018, http://www.ign.com/boards/.

12. Alexander van Engelen, interview with Jono Bacon via forum private message, May 10, 2018.

13. "Kubernetes/Kubernetes: Production-Grade Container Scheduling and Management," GitHub, accessed March 2, 2019, https://github.com/kubernetes/kubernetes.

14. Gilbert Schacter et al., *Psychology* (New York: Worth Publishers, 2011), 295.

15. L. Chapman, and E. Newcomer, "Software Maker Docker Is Raising Funding at $1.3 Billion Valuation," *Bloomberg*, accessed May 10, 2018,

https://www.bloomberg.com/news/articles/2017-08-09/docker
-is-said-to-be-raising-funding-at-1-3-billion-valuation; Red Hat Fact
Sheet, https://investors.redhat.com/~/media/Files/R/Red-Hat
-IR/documents/q218-fact-sheet.pdf; "Red Hat Reports Fourth
Quarter and Fiscal Year 2018 Results," RedHat, March 26, 2018,
https://investors.redhat.com/news-and-events/press-releases
/2018/03-26-2018-211600973.

16. "Tensorflow," GitHub, accessed January 4, 2019, https://github.com
/tensorflow/tensorflow.

17. "TensorFlow Case Studies and Mentions". (n.d.). TensorFlow.
[online] Available at: https://www.tensorflow.org/about/case-studies
[Accessed 29 Mar. 2019].

18. "Ubuntu Search Growth," Google Trends, accessed May 25, 2018,
https://trends.google.com/trends/explore?date=2004-01-01%20
2008-01-11&geo=US&q=ubuntu.

19. "AC/DC—Touch Too Much (Official Video)," 4:26, YouTube video,
March 7, 2013, https://www.youtube.com/watch?v=JGftIcp2SC0.

20. "Seasoned Advice," Stack Exchange, accessed May 26, 2018, https://
cooking.stackexchange.com/.

21. "Mathematics," Stack Exchange, https://math.stackexchange.com/;
"Music," Stack Exchange, https://music.stackexchange.com/; and
"Homebrewing," Stack Exchange, https://homebrew.stackexchange
.com/, all accessed May 26, 2018.

22. "Build Anything on Android," Android Developers, accessed May 26,
2018, https://developer.android.com/.

23. "Civilized Discussion," Discourse, accessed May 26, 2018,
https://www.discourse.org/; "Choose Freedom, Choose Fedora," Get
Fedora, accessed May 26, 2018, https://getfedora.org/.

24. Lanco News, "GOP Presidential Hopeful Ted Cruz Gets Booed on
Colbert," 0:31, YouTube video, September 22, 2015,
https://www.youtube.com/watch?v=4NgmpZ2aXtE.

25. Jim Zemlin, email interview with Jono Bacon, November 28, 2018.

26. Zemlin, interview.

3: BUILD IT AND THEY (MAY) COME

1. "Definition of *Value*," Merriam-Webster, accessed November 26, 2018,
https://www.merriam-webster.com/dictionary/value.

4: HUMANS ARE WEIRD

1. Michael I. Norton, Daniel Mochon, and Dan Ariely, *The "IKEA Effect": When Labor Leads to Love*, (working paper, Harvard Business School, 2011), https://www.hbs.edu/faculty/Publication%20Files/11-091.pdf.
2. Daniel Kahneman, *Thinking, Fast and Slow* (New York: Farrar, Straus & Giroux, 2011).
3. Colleen Walsh, "Layers of Choice," *Harvard Gazette*, February 5, 2014, https://news.harvard.edu/gazette/story/2014/02/layers-of-choice /#pq=v10mwP.
4. David Rock, "SCARF: A Brain-Based Model for Collaborating with and Influencing Others," *NeuroLeadership Journal*, June 15, 2008, http://web.archive.org/web/20100705024057/http://www.your-brain -at-work.com/files/NLJ_SCARFUS.pdf.
5. Rock, "SCARF."

5: CREATE AN INCREDIBLE ADVENTURE

1. Ben Sillis, "The Greatest Video Game Opening Levels of All Time," Red Bull, October 5, 2016, https://www.redbull.com/us-en/the -greatest-ever-video-game-opening-levels.
2. "H.O.G. Members Site," Harley-Davidson, accessed January 9, 2019, https://members.hog.com/.
3. "The Organizer Guide," Meetup, accessed January 8, 2019, https://help .meetup.com/hc/en-us/categories/115000229871-The-Organizer-Guide.
4. "Search: Good First Issue," GitHub, accessed January 5, 2019, https://github.com/search?q=good-first-issue&type=Issues.
5. Antoine de Saint-Exupéry, *The Airman's Odyssey* (New York: Mariner Books, 1984), 39.
6. "Adventures," Fitbit, accessed January 15, 2019, https://www.fitbit .com/challenges/adventures.
7. "2019 Event Schedule," Jeep Jamboree USA, accessed January 15, 2019, https://jeepjamboreeusa.com/tripsregister/.
8. "Top Questions," Stack Overflow, accessed January 15, 2019, https:// stackoverflow.com/?tab=interesting.
9. "Mentors," APS Physics, accessed January 15, 2019, https://www.aps .org/programs/minorities/nmc/mentors.cfm.
10. "Ubuntu Open Week," Ubuntu Wiki, last updated March 18, 2014, https://wiki.ubuntu.com/UbuntuOpenWeek.

11. "How Long Does It Take to Form a Habit? (Backed by Science)," James Clear, accessed November 26, 2018, https://jamesclear.com /new-habit.

12. Nick Saint, "If You're Not Embarrassed by the First Version of Your Product, You've Launched Too Late," *Business Insider*, November 13, 2009, https://www.businessinsider.com/the-iterate-fast-and-release -often-philosophy-of-entrepreneurship-2009-11.

7: GLUE PEOPLE TOGETHER TO CREATE INCREDIBLE THINGS

1. "Miles Davis Quote," AZ Quotes, accessed November 30, 2018, https://www.azquotes.com/quote/636581.

2. Mike Shinoda, email interview with Jono Bacon, October 28, 2018.

3. Ali Velshi, email interview with Jono Bacon, November 3, 2018.

4. Jono Bacon, "Global Learning XPRIZE," Indiegogo, last updated April 9, 2015, https://www.indiegogo.com/projects/global-learning -xprize#/.

5. Richard Read, "Garmin Launches Cryptic Teaser Campaign, We Unravel It, Motor Authority, August 19, 2011, https://www .motorauthority.com/news/1065202_garmin-launches-cryptic -teaser-campaign-we-unravel-it.

6. Virgin Red (@virginred), "What's @richardbranson burying on Necker Island? All will be revealed in just a few short days! #VMarksTheSpot," Twitter, July 25, 2016, 4:21 a.m., https:// twitter.com/VirginRed/status/746634493704929280.

7. "Hack the World 2017," HackerOne, accessed January 10, 2019, https://www.hackerone.com/hacktheworld/2017.

8. Clare Mason, "Light Up the Room With These LED Earrings," Make, May 9, 2018, https://makezine.com/projects/light-room-led-earrings/.

9. "SpreadFirefox," Mozilla Firefox.

8: MOBILIZE YOUR COMMUNITY ARMY

1. John Leyden, "Like My New Wheels? All I Did Was Squash a Bug, and They Gave Me $72k," *The Register*, July 11, 2018, https://www.the register.co.uk/2018/07/11/hackerone_bug_bounty_sitrep/.

2. "Mattermost Security Researcher Mug," Mattermost, accessed January 11, 2019, https://forum.mattermost.org/t/mattermost-security -researcher-mug/1318.

3. Nicole Miller, "Inside Buffer's Community Delight Headquarters: How and Why We Send Swag and What It All Costs," Buffer, last updated June 2, 2015, https://open.buffer.com/community-delight/.

4. Psychestudy. (2018). Yerkes - Dodson Law - Psychestudy. [online] Available at: https://www.psychestudy.com/general/motivation -emotion/yerkes-dodson-law [Accessed 30 Nov. 2018].

5. Gordon-Levitt, interview.

6. Everett, N. (2018). The Story of Twitpic. [online] Medium. Available at: https://medium.com/@noaheverett/the-story-of-twitpic-3c3a 81157c6c [Accessed 30 Mar. 2019].

7. Noah Everett, email interview with Jono Bacon, October 22, 2018.

8. Reddit.com. (2015). Could someone explain how the reddit karma system works? : firstdayontheinternet. [online] Available at: https://www.reddit .com/r/firstdayontheinternet/comments/30b44n/could_someone _explain_how_the_reddit_karma_system/ [Accessed 30 Mar. 2019].

9. Jono Bacon, "First Ubuntu Accomplishments Release," Jono Bacon, May 1, 2012, https://www.jonobacon.com/2012/05/01/first-ubuntu -accomplishments-release/.

9: CYBERSPACE AND MEATSPACE: BETTER TOGETHER

1. SCOREcast, "12th Annual SCOREcast NAMM Meetup," Facebook, January 27, 2018, https://www.facebook.com/events/326049 557801853/.

2. "Community Leadership Summit," accessed January 11, 2019, http://www.communityleadershipsummit.com/.

3. CasinoCoin, "Community Q&A with John Caldwell—CasinoCoin Director of Advocacy," 27:41, YouTube video, August 15, 2018,https:// www.youtube.com/watch?v=b9B5pNN3nu8.

4. Jono Bacon, "Dealing with Disrespect: How to Handle Your Critics, No Matter What They Throw at You," 44:20, YouTube video, November 1, 2014, https://www.youtube.com/watch?v=N5zDHqrFh -M; Jono Bacon, "10 Avoidable Career Mistakes (and How to Conquer Them)," 29:21, YouTube video, October 19, 2018, https://www .youtube.com/watch?v=woEuqMxmJvw.

5. Adobe, "Photoshop Magic Minute," YouTube videos, updated February 26, 2019, https://www.youtube.com/playlist?list=PLXw7EK7 EUaUHcijd8lwc9VP6zC7HaGwTg.

6. Internet Archive, "Ubuntu Developer Summit," Ubuntu, accessed January 12, 2019, https://web.archive.org/web/20121103153904 /http://uds.ubuntu.com/.
7. Jono Bacon, "Keep On Rocking in the Free World," 1:13, YouTube video, November 12, 2011, https://www.youtube.com/watch ?v=dox2nQ3eabg.

10: INTEGRATE, EVOLVE, AND BUILD

1. Whitehurst, interview.
2. "Understanding Discourse Trust Levels," Discourse, June 25, 2018, https://blog.discourse.org/2018/06/understanding-discourse-trust -levels/.

Index